The King Site

The King Site

Continuity and Contact in Sixteenth-Century Georgia

Edited by Robert L. Blakely

The University of Georgia Press   Athens and London

© 1988 by the University of Georgia Press
Athens, Georgia 30602
All rights reserved
Designed by Mary Mendell
Set in Trump Medieval
The paper in this book meets the guidelines for
permanence and durability of the Committee on
Production Guidelines for Book Longevity of the
Council on Library Resources.
Printed in the United States of America
92 91 90 89 88   5 4 3 2 1
Library of Congress Cataloging in Publication Data

The King site.

   Bibliography: p.
   Includes index.
      1. King Site (Ga.) 2. Indians of North America—
Georgia—First contact with Occidental civilization.
3. Spaniards—Georgia—Antiquities. 4. Indians of
North America—Georgia—Antiquities. 5. Georgia—
Antiquities. 6. Excavations (Archaeology)—Georgia.
I. Blakely, Robert L.
F294.K54K56 1988   975.8'01   88-1338
ISBN 0-8203-1039-5 (alk. paper)
ISBN 0-8203-1078-6 (pbk.: alk. paper)

British Library Cataloging in Publication Data available.

Contents

Contents

Figures

Tables

Tables

Introduction

Robert L. Blakely   This book was born during a symposium held at the 1984 meeting of the Southern Anthropological Society in Atlanta. The participants and the audience both received it so enthusiastically that I decided to publish the papers. All agreed that conceptually and topically the work would constitute a significant departure from many edited volumes with similar origins. It differs conceptually in that the collected articles of a volume intended as a reader are seldom so tightly integrated. In this case the focus is biocultural adaptation of native Americans from the King site at the time of European contact, and the story of these people is so compelling—historically and anthropologically—that it demands to be told.

The King site, a sixteenth-century village in northwestern Georgia, formed part of the chiefdom of Coosa. Excavations and archaeological analyses were undertaken in the 1970s, first by Patrick Garrow, then of Shorter College, and later by David Hally of the University of Georgia with grants from the National Geographic Society and the National Endowment for the Humanities. Bioanthropological research was conducted between 1983 and 1987 at Georgia State University under the direction of Robert Blakely and Antoinette Brown, with funding from the National Science Foundation.

The archaeological investigation unearthed a number of European artifacts at the site, most notably iron celts and a basket-hilt sword. The sword, dating to the mid-1500s, was manufactured in Germany or northern Italy but was undoubtedly brought to the Americas by the Spaniards. Historic records indicate that the Iberian explorers most likely to have visited the King site were Hernando de Soto and his army in 1540 and a detachment of soldiers sent by Tristán de Luna in 1560. Moreover, human skeletal remains recovered at the site exhibit animal bite marks associated with fatal wounds inflicted by edged metal weapons.

The King site thus offers the first direct evidence in the interior Southeast of a conflict between a native American community and the Spanish. David Mathews in chapter 8 of this volume concludes that the fatal wounds and bite marks resulted from a battle involving Hernando de Soto's expeditionary force and Coosa Indians (along with Tascaluza's). The bites, according to Mathews, were made by rats and possums that gnawed the corpses between the time of death and interment in the village.

A decade of field and laboratory research has uncovered other unique and important aspects of the site's occupation. Why, for example, at the height of agricultural exploitation in chiefdoms of the Southeast, did our biological data—levels of trace elements, cortical bone thickness, dentition—indicate a diet rich in meat, nuts, and wild grains and cereals? Such an interpretation makes sense when one views the site as a functionally distinct but structurally interrelated socioeconomic unit of the redistributional system comprising the Coosa chiefdom (see Blakely and Brown 1985).

These findings, along with others detailed in the present volume, attest to the problem-solving power of the bioarchaeological approach. Buikstra (1972, 1977) defined bioarchaeology as the explication of past behavior (and particularly of mortuary activity) through the joint efforts of biological anthropologists and archaeologists. The present book, by combining bioanthropological and archaeological hypothesis testing, demonstrates that bioarchaeological analyses are more valuable than analyses by one subdiscipline that tackles problems singly.

Although the overall research design mandated collaboration, the specific questions asked in the laboratory were addressed independently. At the start of the laboratory phase of the project, I called together the student researchers to explain our goals, the procedures, and the allocation of responsibilities for areas of inquiry; I purposely did not suggest how the various interpretations might dovetail. I did not discourage communication, but neither did I tell the researchers how I hoped the results could be integrated. As a result the students felt frustrated but were eager to think of ways in which to piece the puzzle together themselves.

More important, the "double-blind" results made it possible to check the findings independently, so that data from one area did not bias interpretations in another. For example, while Detweiler-Blakely collected information on periosteal reactions, the bones' healing response to malnutrition, infections, and trauma (Steinbock 1976; Ortner and Putschar 1981), Mathews examined the prevalence of healed wounds. The independently analyzed data eventually yielded the anticipated results: cases of periostitis correlated positively with healed wounds. The association was real rather than an artifact of expectation.

This book is not about research design or methodology, however. Nor is it a treatment of statistics. Simple statistical procedures are used when appropriate—usually to test the relationship between classes of variables or the independence or dependence of samples—but they have been kept to a minimum. More-complex tests were also avoided, not because they are inappropriate to the data analyzed, but because they were not crucial to the goal of the present work: a preliminary illumination of the biocultural processes at work at the King site.

The volume is broadly divided into three parts: social life; stress, diet, and disease; and the Spanish encounter. The first section explores the settlement pattern at the King site, the life cycle of the village's inhabitants, the acquisition and expressions of status at the site, the social organization within the community, and its relationship to other groups in the region. David Hally reconstructs the settlement pattern and relates it to the settlement plans of geographically and temporally contiguous peoples. He finds that the perimeter ditch, wooden stockade encircling a domestic zone of summer and winter houses, and central plaza with ceremonial structures, chunky post, and slave post suggest parallels with Upper Creek towns of the eighteenth century. According to Hally, architectural features indicate that the site was occupied briefly—"probably less than fifty years"—a crucial fact that spurred researchers to seek causes for the seemingly premature and precipitous abandonment of the village.

Robert Blakely examines adaptive and maladaptive aspects of the life cycle of King's residents. Using paleodemographic and archaeological data to assess levels of fertility and mortality, he identifies the highest at-risk groups: infants who had yet to develop immunities to infectious diseases, children facing the deleterious consequences of weaning, women of childbearing age, and the elderly. Blakely also notes that mortality was disproportionately high among young adult females and middle-aged men and women, a fact critical to Mathews's reconstruction of the Spanish massacre of King's people. In so doing, his work obliquely addresses the problems and prospects of paleodemographic research. King, a single-component site of short duration, introduces the problem of stochastic perturbations within one or two generations. On the other hand, it lessens the need to control for long-term population growth or decline. Such deviations from the model of population stationarity often confound paleodemographic interpretations (see Johansson and Horowitz 1986 for a discussion).

Marshaling demographic data, burial location, and grave furniture, John Garrett outlines evidence that status among King's occupants was both earned and inherited. Moreover, men of different status could achieve positions in a warrior class. He posits that membership in the warrior class was symbolized by grave goods that included caches of projectile points, penis bones from bears, and red ochre, which for historic Creek Indians represented the blood of their enemies (Swanton 1922). More problematic is Garrett's assertion that artificial cranial deformation constituted a badge of ascriptive status. He nevertheless raises an issue that deserves further study at King and elsewhere.

Lisa Crowder argues that the roots of King social order and settlement pattern can be traced to an amalgamation of the prehistoric Mouse Creek and Dallas cultures to the north in Tennessee. By accepting Lewis and Kneberg's (1955) proposal that Mouse Creek represents an intrusion of Middle Cumberland people into Dallas territory, Crowder neatly explains the presence of elements of all three cultures at King and other Barnett-phase sites in the area. And like Hally, she sees in King's social organization and settlement plan antecedents of the eighteenth-century Upper Creek towns of northern Alabama and Georgia. For Crowder, then, the King site serves as a vital link between the prehistoric and historic inhabitants of the region.

After considering social organization and cultural affiliation the volume turns to subsistence patterns, diet, and stress. There are a number of nonspecific stress indicators of the human skeleton. Usually these indexes do not tell the investigator *what* the stressors were, but they often measure *levels* of stress. When information is also available from other sources, however, it sometimes becomes possible to identify the stressors. The incidence of generalized periostitis, for example, may reveal the prevalence and severity of stress, while trace element levels in bone may suggest the cause, often a dietary imbalance or a chronic disease (Schroeder, Tipton, and Nason 1972; Wing and Brown 1979; Gilbert 1985). In the second part of this volume, the authors assess levels of stress and their causes at the King site. They find, in general, that King's occupants were a pretty healthy lot.

Sharon Kestle compares tooth wear and frequencies of caries between the sexes at King and between individuals at King and Etowah, a nearby Mississippian town whose residents practiced intensive corn agriculture. King teeth, she discovered, exhibit far fewer caries than Etowah teeth, a finding suggesting that King's residents relied less on corn than did their counterparts at Etowah; the sucrose in corn, like sugar in candy today, leads to decay (Mormann and Muhlemann 1981). In fact, poor dental health is one of many deleterious byproducts of corn domestication (Cassidy 1972; Robbins 1977; Cohen and Armelagos 1984; Rose, Condon, and Goodman 1985; Powell 1985). Kestle also notes that women at King had a significantly higher incidence of caries than men, a finding indicating a dietary difference between males and females. The reason may be a sexual division of labor in food procurement or gender-specific disparities in food allocation. These observations are supported by studies of trace element concentrations (Brown and Blakely 1985) and cortical bone thickness.

In chapter 6, Antoinette Brown compares cortical bone thickness—a sensitive index of nutrient intake (Garn 1966)—in King skeletons and in a sample of nonagricultural remains from California. Follow-up comparisons with preagricultural and agricultural samples from the Georgia coast (Larsen 1982; Blakely and Brown 1985) corroborate the author's initial results: King's occupants experienced suboptimal nutrient intake by comparison with gatherers and hunters but more adequate nutrition than agriculturalists. These findings suggest for King a mixed subsistence economy that combined foraging and food production. And Brown's study confirms Kestle's observation that men suffered less from nutritional stress than women.

It would not be surprising, therefore, to find higher frequencies of periostitis—the bones' response to nutritional insult and to other things—for females than for males at King. The contrary proved to be the case. Bettina Detweiler-Blakely in her article reports that the incidence of periosteal reactions is most strongly correlated with individuals Mathews identified as having been wounded, but not killed, in battle with the Spaniards. When the survivors are removed from the sample with periostitis, the prevalence of the condition becomes quite low, suggesting that neither nutritional inadequacy nor infectious disease was sufficient to induce widespread periosteal reaction. Because periosteal reactions stand at the nexus of many interconnected stressors, Detweiler-Blakely's analysis offers an overview of biocultural life at King: low levels of infection, generally adequate nutrition, and—except for the victims of Spanish brutality—little trauma.

The final section of the book examines the ethnohistorical, archaeological, and bioanthropological evidence for placing the Spaniards at the King site in the mid-sixteenth century. That they were close is clear. The European artifacts recovered at the site, coupled with the wounds that edged metal weapons inflicted on the skeletons, are proof. But could the metal implements have been traded in and the wounds inflicted by other Indians who somehow secured the weapons from the Spaniards?

David Mathews brilliantly traces the source of the wounds directly to the Spaniards, specifically to Hernando de Soto's entrada in 1540. He first correlates the distribution of injuries—skulls and leg bones—with the fact that the Spaniards fought "European style," striking the body on heads and legs—those areas left unprotected by armor. He then matches the wounded and killed subsample (young adult females and middle-aged men and women) with the fact that throughout the Coosa chiefdom De Soto took slaves (young women for sexual pleasures and middle-aged people as burden bearers; Bourne 1904). Using the evidence of bite marks and De Soto's chronicles, Mathews implicates the victims in the Battle of Mabila, which took place in south-central Alabama on October 18, 1540. He then speculates that the King site was the village of Ulibahali mentioned in De Soto's chronicles (Bourne 1904).

Charles Hudson, Marvin Smith, and Chester De-Pratter in the final article agree with Mathews that De Soto was the culprit but do so only after eliminating other suspects. However, they dispute the contention that the King site was Ulibahali and question whether the conflict could have occurred as far away as south-central Alabama. Mabila was distant from the King site, and the battered Spaniards were in no mood to have Indian corpses retrieved by their relatives. Weeks would have passed before it was safe for King's residents to retrieve and transport the rotting corpses 190 miles back to King for burial. The authors offer an alternative scenario that puts the massacre in the vicinity of the village. Perhaps the battle casualties interred at King were those who *resisted* enslavement. Hudson, Smith, and DePratter argue that additional information is needed to identify the location of the massacre. They conclude their article with a musing that befits the entire work: "If Sherlock Holmes were summarizing this case to his faithful colleague and companion, he would no doubt say: 'Whatever the King site case is, my dear Watson, it is not elementary.'"

This volume bears witness to our progress in unraveling the mystery. Where do we go from here? Because the questions we are asking are indeed not elementary, we must first secure additional information from the skeletal remains to confirm, alter, or augment our present understanding. Our detailed analyses (now under way) of skeletal dimensions and data derived from teeth, including enamel hypoplasias (see Blakely and Detweiler-Blakely 1987), will provide such information. Archaeological and bioanthropological evidence will enable us to evaluate the impact of European diseases at the site (see

Blakely and Detweiler-Blakely 1985). We can then undertake a *regional* analysis of native American biocultural adaptation at the time of European contact.

It would be impossible to mention all of the people who contributed to this volume, but not to name some would be unthinkable. First, thanks to David Hally, who agreed to lend us the skeletal remains from the King site and then went the extra mile, providing field notes, photographs, burial data sheets, and maps. In bending over backward to meet our research needs, David showed that he pays more than lip service to the importance of multidisciplinary scholarship. I am also grateful to Charles Hudson, who constantly offered encouragement and meticulously compiled information on Spanish expeditions in the sixteenth-century southeastern United States. Charles Merbs, Arizona State University, was helpful in diagnosing bone pathologies. And I thank Lewis H. Larson for loan of the Etowah skeletons.

To the student researchers who dedicated themselves to the tedium of data collection as well as the exhilaration of discovery, I owe a special debt of gratitude. This volume would never have been published without the diligence and conscientious efforts of Lisa Crowder, Bettina Detweiler-Blakely, John Garrett, Sharon Kestle, and David Mathews. Rick Woodworth and Karen Oates, although joining the project too late to write articles, nonetheless contributed significantly to the research.

Lane Beck of Harvard University and the Peabody Museum critically reviewed an earlier draft of this manuscript. The volume is better for her cogent comments. I also thank two anonymous readers for their many helpful suggestions. The responsibility for any errors that remain, however, rests solely with me. Rebekah Hudgins expertly edited the book for style and content. Bettina Detweiler-Blakely painstakingly prepared the index. Stephen Fievet, Jean Reed, and Anita Williams typed the manuscript. Karen Orchard, associate director and executive editor at the University of Georgia Press, paved the way for publication.

This work was supported by National Science Foundation grants BNS-8217377 and SOC-7503833 and by Georgia State University grant 8504702.

I

Social Life

I

Archaeology and Settlement Plan of the King Site

David J. Hally

The King site is an early historic Indian town located in northwest Georgia approximately twenty-five miles west of the city of Rome (figure 1.1). The site is situated in the floodplain of the Coosa River on the inside bank of a large meander loop known as Foster Bend. The approximately two thousand acres of fertile bottomland surrounding the site constitute one of the largest tracts of alluvial land in the northwestern part of the state.

Scientific investigation of the King site began in 1971 when Patrick Garrow, then instructor of anthropology at Shorter College, commenced weekend excavations with a volunteer crew. Intensive investigations of the site were conducted by the University of Georgia for a nine-month period between December 1973 and September 1974. Research during this period was directed by Garrow and the author and was supported by local contributions and grants from the National Geographic Society, the National

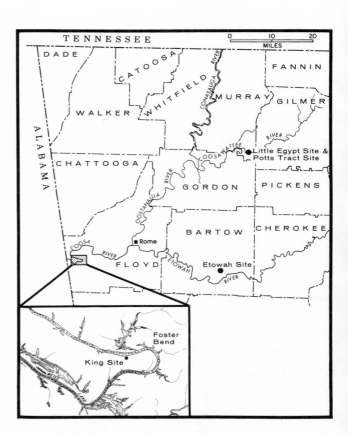

Figure 1.1
Location of the King
site in northwest
Georgia

Endowment for the Humanities, and the University of Georgia.

The King site covers approximately five acres. Nearly two-thirds of the site, or 112,000 square feet, have been excavated. The remaining portion was not available for excavation at the time of intensive investigation in 1974.

Stratigraphically, the site consists of light-colored sandy loam subsoil and an overlying plow zone. Occupation refuse and virtually all of the aboriginal occupation surface have been destroyed by cultivation and by overbank erosion from the Coosa River. Features such as burials and postmolds, however, are

4

preserved in the subsoil and are easily detected. Contours of the subsoil surface and the relative absence of features along the southern periphery of the site indicate that erosion damage is greatest in the southwestern corner of the excavated area. Subsoil is as much as two feet lower in the southwestern corner than it is farther north and east. Structures with intact floors were found only along the eastern edge of the site.

Excavation of the site entailed first the removal of the plow zone and the exposure of subsoil surface. Heavy earth-moving equipment was used extensively in this operation. Features appearing on the exposed subsoil surface were mapped with plane table and alidade and, with the exception of postmolds, were subsequently excavated by hand. Altogether, 213 burials, seven intact house floors, and a small number of miscellaneous features were excavated.

For all practical purposes, the King site is a single-component site. This component has its closest cultural affiliation with the late Lamar occupations at the Potts Tract and Little Egypt sites located fifty miles upstream at Carters Dam (Hally 1970, 1979). Artifactual and architectural styles are so similar among these components that all can be assigned to the Barnett phase. Research dealing with mid-sixteenth-century Spanish expeditions into the interior Southeast has led Hudson et al. (*Chiefdom*, 1985) to identify the Barnett phase and the Dallas–Mouse Creek phases of the upper Tennessee River valley with the province of Coosa. The available ethnohistoric and archaeological evidence suggests that Little Egypt was the capital of this province. If these identifications are correct, the inhabitants of the King site spoke a Muskogean language and were ancestral to some of the eighteenth-century Upper Creek towns of northeastern Alabama.

Radiocarbon dates indicate that the Barnett phase was in existence during most of the sixteenth century. A more accurate date for the King site occupation is provided by European artifacts that were recovered from several burials. These artifacts include iron celts, knives and chisels (Smith 1975), and a basket-hilt sword (figures 1.2 and 1.3). The sword was found by pot hunters after University of Georgia excavations and has been dated to the mid-sixteenth century by Helmut Nickel of the Metropolitan Museum of Art in New York. It was manufactured in either Germany or northern Italy.

The basic elements of the King site settlement plan are: (1) a defensive perimeter consisting of a ditch and palisade; (2) an inner zone of domestic structures; and (3) a large, centrally located plaza

Figure 1.2
European-manufactured iron chisels, celts, and knife recovered in native American burials at the King site. The scale is in centimeters.

Figure 1.3
Basket hilt of a
Spanish sword found
at the King site

containing buildings and other architectural features of a presumably public and ceremonial nature
(figure 1.4).

The ditch that encircles the entire excavated portion of the site is somewhat variable in cross section
but tends to have a flat bottom and steeply sloping
sides. At the time of construction, it would have had
a depth of at least four to five feet and a bottom
width of eight to eleven feet. There is no stratigraphic evidence that it ever held water. At no place in the
exposed length of the ditch has evidence of an elevated crossing been encountered.

Magnatometer survey and test excavations in the
unexcavated portion of the site in 1975 provided evidence of the ditch and its configuration on the
town's western perimeter (figure 1.5). This evidence
makes it possible to characterize the overall configuration of the aboriginal town:

1. The town was bounded by a ditch on three sides
   and by the Coosa River on the fourth.

Figure 1.4
Map of the King site
excavation, showing
postholes, burials, and
ditch

8

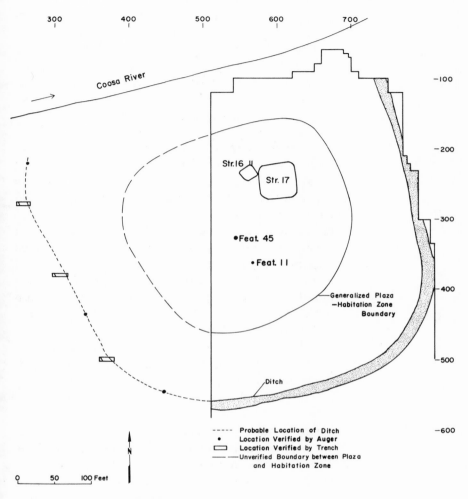

300   400   500   600   700

Coosa River

−100

−200

Str. 16

Str. 17

−300

•Feat. 45

•Feat. 11

Generalized Plaza
—Habitation Zone
Boundary

−400

−500

Ditch

N

0   50   100 Feet

- - - - - Probable Location of Ditch
•   Location Verified by Auger
▭   Location Verified by Trench
—— Unverified Boundary between Plaza
       and Habitation Zone

−600

Figure 1.5
Map of the King site, showing location of the ditch on the west side

9

2. The area enclosed by the ditch is roughly square, measuring 480 feet east-west and 460 feet north-south.
3. The river bank and eastern and southern ditch lines form three sides of a nearly perfect square that is oriented 17 degrees off the cardinal directions. The western ditch line is oriented 26 degrees off the cardinal directions.

Throughout most of its exposed length, the palisade is represented by a single line of posts spaced an average of 1.5 feet apart. The distance between palisade and ditch varies between 10 and 20 feet. Architectural features such as bastions and entrances are difficult to recognize and could be absent, at least in the area exposed. What may be a screened entrance and associated bastion are located east of Structure 22 (S390–420 E780–790 in figure 1.4). Small semicircular posthole arrangements measuring 7 feet by 4 feet occur at two points (S280 E770 and S495 E710) along the palisade and could represent bastions. These features in size and shape approach the bastions associated with one of the palisade lines at the Jonathan Creek site in Kentucky (Webb 1952:10).

In two locations (S220 E760 and S460 E770), posthole lines extending in excess of thirty feet occur between and parallel to the ditch and palisade. These may be remnants of an earlier palisade destroyed as a result of ditch construction. Finally, lines of posts in several locations may be attributed to palisade repair.

A domestic habitation zone, measuring 80–120 feet in width, lies adjacent to the palisade. Two types of features—human burials and postmolds—occur with great frequency in this zone. Postmold patterns representing twenty-five habitation structures and at least nine open-sided sheds or granaries can be identified among the latter (figure 1.4). Assuming that the domestic habitation zone is of relatively uniform width throughout the site and that the density of houses in that zone is relatively uniform, it is possible to estimate the total number of habitation structures present in the town at forty-seven.

The general characteristics of habitation structures include: (1) floors that are depressed one to two feet below ground surface; (2) single-post wall construction; (3) wall-trench entry passages located at building corners; (4) floor plans that are rectangular with rounded corners; (5) four interior roof support posts; and (6) central hearths (figure 1.6). Structures range in size between nineteen and thirty-one feet and are often exactly square. Exterior walls were probably of wattle-and-daub construction, although there is some evidence that perishable materials such as thatch, bark, or woven mats were also used. Earth from the excavated house basin was probably banked against the exterior of these walls. Roofs were probably peaked and covered with thatch or bark. This type of structure is characteristic of Lamar culture throughout northern Georgia (Hally 1986), and Dallas (Polhemus 1985) and Mouse Creek (Sullivan 1987) cultures in eastern Tennessee.

The majority of habitation structures appear to have been dismantled and rebuilt at least once. Typically the entire structure was shifted one or two feet from its original position at the time of rebuilding. In several instances, the number of hearths exceeds the number of wall-building stages, indicating perhaps an intermediate step in the life cycle of a domestic structure.

The floor area of habitation structures was apparently divided into several distinct activity areas. The four interior support posts define a central zone that

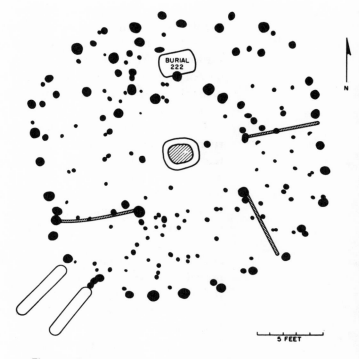

Figure 1.6
Plan of a domestic structure at the King site, showing hearth, wall-trench entry, and clay partition walls

contains the hearth but few postmolds and little oc-cupation debris. Presumably cooking and socializing occurred here. Postmolds of small diameter are com-mon in the outer floor zone. These probably served as bench or bed supports and as partition walls but may have had other functions as well. Raised benches placed against exterior walls were a com-mon feature of native American houses throughout the Southeast in the historic period (Swanton 1946:422). Evidence that the postmolds indicate par-titions is provided by preserved basal remnants of clay and post walls in two structures.

Domestic refuse, in the form of potsherds, stone debitage, animal bone, and charred plant material, was heavily concentrated in the southern half of structures with preserved floors (Structures 4, 5/10, 7, 8, 9, 14, and 23) but was virtually absent in the northern half of the same structures. This situation contrasts markedly with the distribution of subfloor burials, which were found almost exclusively in the northern half of structures. Since ethnohistoric evidence indicates that southeastern Indians buried some of their dead beneath the beds of the living (Williams 1930:187; Swanton 1946:724), we may hypothesize that beds were located primarily against the northern walls of habitation structures. If trash tended to accumulate where it was produced, the north-south distribution of occupational debris may indicate that sleeping and general household maintenance activities were separated within each structure.

The arrangement of habitation structures within the domestic zone seems to have been affected by at least two factors. First, in orientation each structure usually conforms to the compass orientation of the adjacent palisade section. Second, adjacent structures are frequently grouped around small courtyards between forty and sixty feet square. Particularly clear examples include Structures 2, 4, and 9; Structures 7, 8, and 23; and Structures 6, 11, 13, and 15 (figure 1.4). The habitation structures surrounding a courtyard and opening onto it were probably occupied by the members of a single extended family. Similar courtyard arrangements are described for the eighteenth-century Creeks (Swanton 1928:172). In two instances—Structures 3 and 4—habitation structures appear to have been crowded into small, marginal areas. They may have been later additions to the extended-family household.

Generally speaking, the space between habitations is relatively free of postmolds. When postmolds are present, they tend to occur in small clusters adjacent to habitations or in the center of courtyards. These clusters usually have a rectangular configuration that measures ten to nineteen feet long and six to fourteen feet wide. An especially clear example occurs at N285 E700 (figure 1.4). They apparently represent either open-sided sheds used for domestic activities during the summer or granaries with raised floors for the storage of corn and other foodstuffs. Similar structures are reported from the Dallas-culture Toqua site on the Little Tennessee River (Polhemus 1985).

The plaza, a large area in the center of the site which is characterized by a low density of postmolds, measures 300 feet north-south and probably 240 feet east-west. Notable features within the plaza are the two large pits, Features 11 and 45, and Structures 16 and 17. Feature 45 is a circular pit measuring 3.5 feet in diameter and 5 feet in depth. It is located almost exactly in the center of the site (figure 1.5). Feature 11 is a narrower but equally deep circular pit 1.5 feet in diameter. Both features are unique on the site and are no doubt postholes. Given their size and location, it is possible that the posts they held can be identified as the "chunky" and "slave" posts that have been described for late eighteenth-century Creek towns (Swanton 1928:188–190). Both kinds of posts stood in the town plaza, or "chunky yard." Chunky posts were 30 to 40 feet tall, measured 2 to 3 feet across at the base, and were used in a ball game played between men and women. Slave posts stood about 12 feet high and were used for the display of scalps and the torture of war captives (Swanton 1928:188–190).

Structure 17, measuring forty-eight feet square, is by far the largest building discovered at the King site (figure 1.5). The central floor area of the structure is bounded by eight interior support posts and contains a hearth. The only indication of an entrance are two paired wall posts at the southeast corner of the structure.

Structure 17 probably had public and ceremonial functions and may well have been similar to the Creek "hot house," or communal men's house. This structure is described in the eighteenth-century literature as round or square with round corners. The interior postmold alignments probably represent supports for platforms which were a common feature of Creek community structures.

Immediately adjacent to Structure 17 on the west is Structure 16, a building which in nearly all respects is similar to the habitation structures described above. It differs only in location, the absence of burials, and the presence of a small pit containing a pottery vessel located immediately south of the hearth. The function of this structure is not known. However, given its location, it probably played a role in community affairs.

Our investigation encompassed 213 burials in the excavated portion of the site. These were distributed throughout the excavated area, although the overwhelming majority (185) occurred in the domestic zone. In this area, 97 burials occurred inside habitations, and 88 occurred in the space between habitations. In the latter location, burials were frequently placed beneath the structures identified as sheds or granaries. In the plaza, 10 burials occurred in Structure 17, one was located south of the large post pits, and 19 occurred in two clusters located north of Structures 16 and 17. Grave goods associated with the plaza burials suggest that they represent high-status individuals (Seckinger 1977).

The dominant mode of burial is that of a lightly flexed inhumation. With the exception of nine pits containing two bodies and four pits containing three to six bodies, single interment is the rule.

Architectural evidence indicates that the King site was occupied for a relatively brief period of time, probably less than fifty years. David Mathews (see chapter 8) raises the possibility that inhabitants of the site had direct and violent contact with European explorers, presumably Spanish. The fact that most of the seven excavated habitation structures were destroyed by fire would seem to support the possibility that the King site was abandoned as a result of that encounter. It should be noted, however, that site abandonment almost certainly did not take place at the time of initial Spanish contact. All five burials containing European artifacts reflect traditional interment, and three of the individuals were interred within habitation structures. We may infer that the village was occupied for at least a short time after the initial Spanish contact.

David J. Hally

16

2

**The Life Cycle
and Social
Organization**

Robert L. Blakely

Paleodemography is a useful tool for mortuary site archaeology. Following the pioneering work of Vallois (1960), Angel (1969), Acsádi and Nemeskéri (1970), Weiss (1973, 1975, 1976), Asch (1976), Howell (1976), Swedlund and Armelagos (1976), Palkovich (1978), and Van Gerven and Armelagos (1983), paleodemographic analyses of skeletal populations are being used today to reconstruct fertility, fecundity, morbidity, mortality, population size, population growth, episodic and epidemic diseases, and social organization. In this chapter I use paleodemography (1) to help reconstruct the health environment of the occupants of the King site; (2) to propose the fundamental principles of social organization at the site; and (3), as in the King site research project, to suggest hypotheses that may be tested by other means of bioarchaeological analysis.

In the earliest archaeological account of the site, Margaret C. Ashley stated that the "culture of the site was like that of Etowah" (Moorehead 1932:157).

Subsequent investigations at King, while confirming Ashley's overall impression, have also linked the site—at least ceramically—with the Potts Tract and Little Egypt sites (Hally 1970), located some fifty miles to the northeast (Hally 1975b). And certain similarities (as well as differences) have been noted with the early historic occupations of Weiss and Guntersville reservoirs in northeastern Alabama (Hally 1975b).

A number of features of the King site are noteworthy for present purposes. The site consists of a single component radiocarbon dated between A.D. 1410 and 1830 (Geochronology Laboratory, University of Georgia). Using cross-dating, Hally has placed the occupation between A.D. 1550 and 1725 (Hally 1975b). Because the stockade received only limited repair and there is little crowding of architectural features, Hally believes that the site was inhabited briefly—"probably less than fifty years" (1975c:15). The settlement was surrounded by the Coosa River and a dry moat, within which stood a wooden palisade. Rectangular dwellings occupy the space between the fortification and a centrally located plaza with ceremonial buildings (Hally, Garrow, and Trotti 1975). Seckinger (1977) has divided the site into two distinct functional areas: a private sector, including the domestic structures and environs, and a public sector, including the plaza and ceremonial structures (figure 2.1).

Various studies have been made of the King settlement pattern and architecture (Garrow 1975) and of European artifacts recovered on the site (Smith 1975). Preliminary attempts have also been made to describe the roughly two hundred excavated skeletons (Tally 1975; Funkhouser 1978). Tally (1975) in an examination of a portion of the sample found an "unusually high" incidence of deaths among indi-

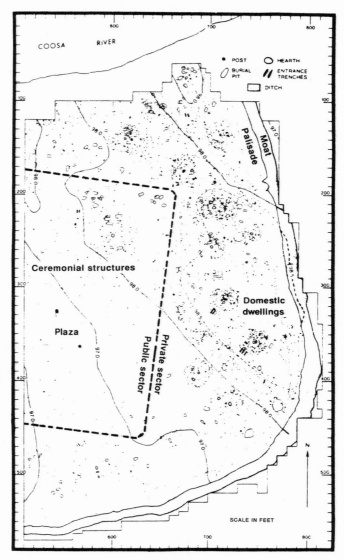

Figure 2.1
Layout of the
excavated portion of
the King site,
illustrating public and
private sectors.
Adapted from Hally
1975a:50.

viduals between the ages of eighteen and thirty and speculated that European diseases may have been the cause. Funkhouser (1978) disputes this interpretation, arguing that the apparently differential mortality actually reflects selective inclusion or exclusion of age classes in the public and private sectors. He held (erroneously, I believe) that adult males and children alone were included in public burials, with adult females and adult males up to thirty years of age totally absent. Funkhouser interpreted this finding to mean that the King interments represented both earned and inherited status. He notes: "Based on an analysis of grave goods, Seckinger (1977) hypothesized a combination of ascribed and achieved status for the King society. Blakely (1977) reached a similar conclusion concerning Etowah social structure. We might hypothesize, therefore, that this represents a general pattern of sociocultural adaptation that existed during certain phases of the Mississippian period in northwestern Georgia" (Funkhouser 1978:69–70).

Materials and Methods

The present chapter reflects the analysis of 189 recoverable skeletons. (An appendix to this volume lists all analyzed skeletons and indicates assigned ages and sexes, burial location [public or private sector], wounded survivors and individuals killed in battle with the Spaniards, and individuals bearing animal bite marks and evidence of periosteal reactions.) The validity of the interpretations of demographic data depends partly on the ability of the researcher to determine age and sex accurately. It is important neither to skew ages consistently toward one end of the age continuum nor to bias sex assignment systematically, a frequent albeit unintentional practice among both inexperienced and experienced investigators (Weiss 1972; Buikstra and Mielke 1985). Sexual dimorphism in the King site sample was great enough to ensure accurate identification of the sex of adults and adolescents (see Thieme and Schull 1957; Birkby 1966; Phenice 1969; Hamilton 1975). Although 56 percent of the remains were female and 44 percent male, a chi-square test indicated that this difference does not deviate significantly from the expected 1 : 1 sex ratio.

To determine age at death, multiple criteria were applied discriminately whenever possible to achieve maximum accuracy. Subadolescents were assigned ages on the basis of calcification and eruption of deciduous and permanent dentition (Schour and Massler 1944; Dahlberg and Menegaz-Bock 1958; Moorrees, Fanning, and Hunt 1963a, 1963b), linear length of long bones (Merchant and Ubelaker 1977; Hoffman 1979), and ossification and fusion of bony elements such as the neural arches of the vertebrae (Bass 1971). These age indicators are generally assumed to substantiate each other, and they usually do, but in some instances contradictory evidence makes age assessment more difficult. In these cases, dental development and eruption were regarded as the most reliable criteria of skeletal age for subadolescents (Johnston 1969).

The ages of adolescents were determined from epiphyseal union (we took into account sex differences in the rate of maturation; Stewart and Trotter 1954) and eruption of the permanent dentition (Schour and Massler 1944; Dahlberg and Menegaz-Bock 1958; Moorrees, Fanning, and Hunt 1963b). According to Krogman (1962), the pubic symphysis is the most reliable age indicator beyond nineteen years. In this study, too, age changes in the symphyseal face were considered the most accurate and consistent measures of age and were regarded as decisive when discrepancies arose; McKern and Stewart's (1957) criteria were employed for males and Gilbert and McKern's (1973) criteria were used for females (see also Suchey 1979). Epiphyseal union (Stewart and Trotter 1954), dental attrition (Brothwell 1965), and endocranial suture closure (Todd and Lyon 1925; Singer 1953)—when corroborated by other evidence or when they were the only available criterion—were also employed to determine the ages of individuals beyond twenty years.

Demographic theory requires that populations be stable; that is, they must be of large size, with no migration and constant rates of growth based on unchanging age-specific fertility and mortality (Weiss 1976). The population is not assumed to be stationary, or to have a zero growth rate. The group can experience either positive or negative growth, but the trend must persist over generations (Underwood 1979).[1] While it is theoretically possible to ascertain stability in living populations, it is virtually impossible to do so in skeletal series. However, Weiss (1973) reports that if the mortality curve approximates a pyramid—that is, if more deaths appear in the middle range of the potential life span—then one can assume that the sample approaches stability.

Figure 2.2 compares the mortality profiles of a Mississippian sample from Dickson Mounds, Illinois, and the skeletal series from the King site (Blakely 1971). The Dickson Mounds curve is pyramidal, indicating age stability. The King site adult profile, on the other hand, is bimodal, suggesting monumental perturbations in age structure. In closed populations, according to demographic theory, such perturbations result from sampling error, changes in the fertility rate, or differential mortality

Figure 2.2
Mortality profiles of
the King site skeletal
sample (sexes com-
bined, N = 189) and
Dickson Mounds Mis-
sissippian skeletal
sample (sexes com-
bined, N = 479)

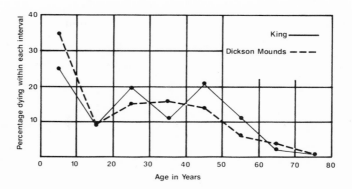

due to profound sociocultural disruptions such as warfare, famine, or epidemic diseases (Weiss 1975, 1976). In the case of the King site, sampling error and sociocultural trauma are implicated.

Results and Discussion

Figure 2.3 divides King site mortality into ten-year intervals according to gender. The shaded portions of the age cohorts represent those segments of the burial population that Mathews (1984a, 1984b) found to have been killed in battle with a Spanish expeditionary party. When these individuals are removed from the total sample, the profile more closely approaches a pyramid. And because the known battle casualties probably represent only the tip of the iceberg, a greater smoothing of the curve would probably be evident if more of the victims were identifiable and removed from the mortality profile. (See chapter 8.)

The other major problem with King site mortality—clearly involving sampling error—is the underrepresentation of small infants in the skeletal sample. Only 1 percent of the burial population was under one year of age at death, as compared with 10 percent in the Etowah village sample (Blakely and Mathews 1975) and 15 percent among Dickson

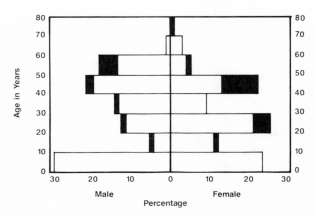

Figure 2.3
Percentages of males (N = 83) and females (N = 106) who died within ten-year intervals for the King site sample. Proportions are based on 100 percent for each sex. Subadolescent percentages presuppose equal numbers of male and female deaths. The shaded portions indicate individuals killed in battle with the Spaniards.

Mounds Mississippians (Blakely 1971). These deaths at Etowah and Dickson are attributable in large measure to fertility schedules, to infant mortality in the absence of modern medical technology, and to the loss of immunity to disease initially conferred upon the fetus by its mother.

First-year mortality at the King site, if we rely solely on skeletal evidence, was less than that in the United States in 1986. There are three possible explanations for the dearth of infants. (1) Separate cemeteries may have been established for the very young; (2) fertility may have been unusually low; and (3) neonatal and infant remains may not have been preserved to the same extent as those of other age groups. Given the archaeological recovery of a few young infants from the site, it seems unlikely that there were separate cemeteries. Similarly, the frequent occurrence of gestation pits and pre-auricular sulci on the female pelvis—indications of childbirth (Stewart 1970; Houghton 1974; Ullrich 1975; Ashworth et al. 1976; Suchey et al. 1979)—argue against the second alternative (Oates 1987). Differential preservation therefore seems to be the most plausible explanation. Garrow (1984) observed that the graves of infants were shallower than those of older individuals, so that they would have been more susceptible to destruction from plowing and erosion.

We may logically ask about the effect that the underrepresentation of infants and large number of battle casualties exerted on the mortality statistics. The mean age at death for the King site population was twenty-eight years.[2] This figure compares with twenty-three years in the Etowah village (Blakely and Mathews 1975) and twenty-four years among the Mississippians from Dickson Mounds (Blakely 1971). The battle fatalities did not at all lower the average age at death for the King site; the mean age at death among the known victims was forty years.

The underrepresentation of infants exerted a greater effect on average age at death. If we artificially add 10 percent first-year mortality (the Etowah figure) to the real data, the mean age at death decreases from twenty-eight to twenty-six years. Still, King site mortality was not as great as mortality at Etowah or Dickson and actually more closely approximates that found in less agricultural and relatively more disease-free groups, such as Archaic and Woodland peoples (Blakely 1971). Sattenspiel and Harpending (1983) argue that elevated average skeletal age means a depressed birth rate, but as we have seen, no compelling evidence suggests that such was the case at the King site.

Mortality was elevated at King for individuals at ages three and four years. Fully 52 percent of all subadolescent deaths occurred within this two-year span. (This figure would be lower, of course, if more neonates had been recovered.) It can reasonably be assumed that these fatalities resulted from a partial failure of the weaning program. It was not unusual in aboriginal America for weaning to occur so late, and late weaning may have helped space out births, since lactation inhibits fertility. The same mortality peak was seen in the Etowah village sample (Blakely and Mathews 1975), although there the skeletons in this age group evidenced porotic hyperostosis, a bone condition due either to anemia from abnormal hemoglobins or to protein deficiency (Angel 1969). This we attributed to the transition from high-protein mother's milk to a high-carbohydrate/high-sucrose corn-based diet.

A comparison of the age incidence of enamel hypoplasias between King and the Etowah village offers a second explanation for the elevated mortality and generalized stress observed at this age in the Etowah skeletons. Enamel hypoplasias are macroscopically observable pits or bands that form across the tooth crown as a result of the cessation of ameloblastic activity (figure 2.4). Since ameloblastic activity is tied to metabolic disturbances, enamel defects at specific stages of crown formation indicate age episodes of metabolic perturbations (Pindborg 1970). Investigators have clearly demonstrated an association between enamel hypoplasias and both nutritional stress and systemic disorders (Massler, Schour, and Poncher 1941; El-Najjar, DeSanti, and Ozebek 1978; Goodman, Armelagos, and Rose 1980). With little variation, the correlations with such stresses are high, with r^2 values around .5 (Goodman et al. 1984).

Age incidence of enamel hypoplasias among those surviving to adulthood at King and the Etowah village reveals comparable levels of childhood stress, in

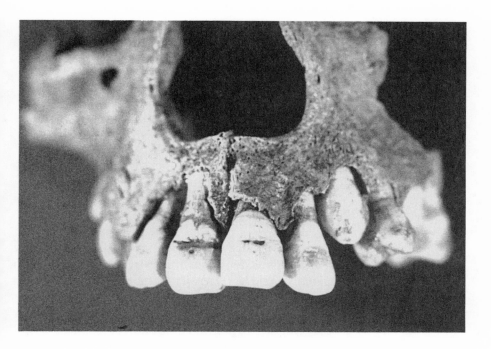

Figure 2.4
Enamel hypoplasias,
an indication of meta-
bolic disturbance, on
the upper central in-
cisors of a nine-year-
old of indeterminate
sex from the Etowah
village (Burial 38)

both groups peaking at about age four (figure 2.5). As children, then, adults at Etowah faced no greater risk of debilitating disease than did King's occupants who lived to maturity. Among individuals who failed to reach adulthood, a different picture emerges. Figure 2.6 shows that while only one in five subadolescent decedents at King experienced severe stress at about 3.5 years—aside from the obvious fact that they were dead—fully half of Etowah's deceased children did. Detweiler-Blakely and I (1985) did not interpret this finding to mean that King's youth were subjected to increased levels of acute diseases, for childhood mortality at King was substantially lower than at Etowah. We believe that Etowah children were "weeded out" rather early on, many at the age of weaning. In addition to the dietary transition, death likely resulted from opportunistic, endemic pathogens supported by

Figure 2.5
Age incidence of
enamel hypoplasias
among adults in the
King site skeletal sam-
ple (solid line, $N = 68$)
and in the Etowah
skeletal sample (bro-
ken line, $N = 31$)

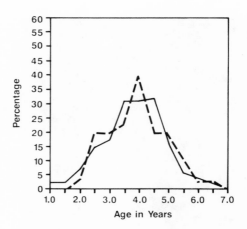

Etowah's greater population density and borne by contaminated food consumed after children had been taken off their relatively pathogen-free lactiferous diet.

Moreover, children aged three to four years old at the King site exhibit no porotic hyperostosis. Therefore, if they were succumbing to nutritional stress occasioned by unsuccessful weaning, it appears not to have involved protein deficiency. Here, then, we may have evidence that subsistence at the King site involved less agriculture and more gathering and hunting than for some other protohistoric southeastern Indians, an idea developed by Sharon Kestle (see chapter 5).

Table 2.1 gives a breakdown of King mortality by ten-year intervals. Most significant are the mortality rate, which, when we hold fertility constant, expresses the probability of dying during any given age interval, and the survivorship rate, which, as the reciprocal of the mortality rate, indicates the likelihood that a person will live through any particular decade.[3] The mortality and survivorship rates show that death was least likely to occur during the teen years. This finding was surprising in light of the fact that we expected to find circumstantial evidence of European diseases in this age group.[4] Because this was a period of depressed mortality in prehistoric America, and because European diseases tended to hit individuals in their late teens and early twenties hardest (Burnet and White 1972), we anticipated higher frequencies of death between ages fifteen and twenty-five. However, the 9 percent mortality in the teen years at King is identical to that of prehistoric Dickson (Blakely 1971) and actually lower than Etowah's 11 percent (Blakely and Mathews 1975). These data offer modest evidence for the absence of European disease at the King site. (See Blakely and Detweiler-Blakely 1985 for a discussion of the behavior of epidemic diseases in virgin-soil populations and the improbability that Old World diseases decimated King's ranks.)

With the exception of fatalities incurred in battle, adult mortality at the King site conforms to a pattern seen in many late prehistoric populations in the eastern United States. Elevated mortality in the twenties can be linked largely to difficulties surrounding childbearing. Excluding battle victims

Figure 2.6
Age incidence of enamel hypoplasias among subadolescents in the King site skeletal sample (solid line, $N = 31$) and in the Etowah skeletal sample (broken line, $N = 19$)

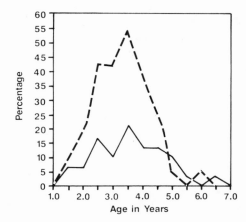

(which were predominantly women), females account for two-thirds of this category.[5] Thus these deaths reflect in large measure the *projected* mortality among neonates. Deaths in the forties and fifties pose no mystery. In addition to death at the hands of the Spaniards, fatalities can be attributed to so-called old-age diseases. The likelihood of dying of any cause in one's forties was more than 60 percent, and the probability of death reached 80 percent in the fifties. The declining number of deaths in the fifties and sixties (figure 2.2) refers not to a lower probability of death but to a reduction in the size of the cohort left to die.

Figure 2.7 compares the mortality profiles of public interments at the King site (high-status individuals buried in and around the ceremonial buildings) and the private remains (low-status individuals inhumed in and around the domestic structures). The high-status burials include slightly more males than females, but a chi-square test indicated that the difference in sex ratio between the high- and low-status burials was not significant. The most striking feature of the two mortality profiles is the degree to

Table 2.1   Frequencies and percentages of deaths, mortality rates, and survivorship rates for the King site sample

Age interval	Frequency	Cumulative frequency	Percentage	Cumulative percentage	Mortality rate	Survivorship rate
0–9	48	48	25	25	.254	.746
10–19	18	66	9	34	.128	.872
20–29	37	103	20	54	.301	.699
30–39	20	123	11	65	.233	.767
40–49	40	163	21	86	.606	.394
50–59	21	184	11	97	.808	.192
60–69	4	188	2	99	.800	.200
70–79	1	189	1	100	1.000	.000

Note: For the sexes combined, $N = 189$.

Figure 2.7
Mortality profiles of
the King site private
sample (sexes
combined, $N = 152$)
and public sample
(sexes combined,
$N = 37$)

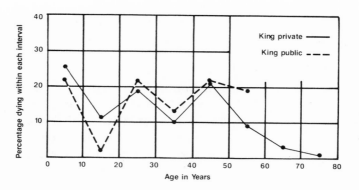

which they are similar. The Smirnov test, a non-parametric test of ordinally scaled variables (Blalock 1972), showed that the age structures of the two segments of King society are not statistically different. The fact that the high-status burial ground includes infants, children, and adults of both sexes suggests that status was ascribed (see Peebles and Kus 1977; Peebles 1983). That is, subadolescents would be accorded interment in the high-status cemetery only if they belonged there by birth; they certainly had little opportunity to rise in status. The possibility remains, however, of upward mobility within and between ascribed segments, a question John Garrett and Lisa Crowder address in chapters 3 and 4.

Figure 2.7 illustrates slightly lower subadolescent mortality in the public sector than in the private sector. This finding translates into an older mean age at death: thirty-one years among public remains and twenty-seven years for the private interments. Perhaps, as in some other hierarchical societies, individuals inheriting high status either experienced lower fertility or received preferential health care treatment and somewhat better nutrition (Haviland 1967; Brown 1973; Hatch and Willey 1974; Schoeninger 1979; Schoeninger and Peebles 1981;

Geidel 1982; Hatch and Geidel 1983; Hatch, Willey, and Hunt 1983). If the latter was the case, data regarding trace elements and enamel hypoplasias do not support it. There are no appreciable differences in concentrations of trace elements or incidences of hypoplasias between members of the two status groups (Brown and Blakely 1985; Detweiler-Blakely 1985).[6] Neither finding contradicts the paleodemographic evidence for ascriptive status at the King site.

Conclusions

This paper has shown, I hope, the utility of paleodemographic analysis for reconstructing the health environment and social organization of the King site—or of any mortuary site with adequate numbers of sufficiently preserved skeletal remains. Skeletons constitute the most direct evidence of population structure—fertility, fecundity, morbidity, and mortality. And population structure stands squarely at the interface between human biology and culture. As Chris Peebles has written, "A human burial contains more anthropological information per cubic meter of deposit than any other type of archeological feature. A burial represents the latent images of a biological and cultural person frozen in a clearly delimited segment of space and time" (Peebles 1977:124).

In the face of legitimate (and illegitimate) demands and legislation for reburial, it is more important than ever that archaeologists secure as large and as representative a sample of the burial population as the excavation program permits. It also means the recovery of every salvable scrap of bone as intact as possible from individual skeletons. Through these procedures, and with biological anthropologists' increasing understanding of population dynamics, old questions will be answered and new questions will be asked.

Notes

1. Johansson and Horowitz (1986) disagree. They found that paleodemographic analyses usually assume stationarity. In stationary populations, birth and death rates are the same, so that mean age at death is equal to life expectancy at birth. For stationary populations, then, data regarding age at death can be used to estimate mortality and fertility. These estimates, in turn, form the empirical basis for hypotheses about the relationship between demographic fluctuations and, say, socioeconomic change. However, because the assumption of stationarity is rarely justified, interpretations based on these demographic parameters are suspect.

2. Mean age at death, as we have seen, cannot usually be equated with life expectancy, which is the number of years one can expect to live beyond a particular age. The actuary tables that insurance companies use today to calculate your premiums are based on life expectancy.

3. Although the mortality rate is a handy mathematical means for expressing the likelihood of death, it may not reflect periods of life-and-death crises that were recognized by the King site residents; the ethnographic evidence from many contemporary societies indicates that deaths among young individuals are more poorly received than deaths among the aged (Driver 1961). The absolute frequencies or the percentages of deaths, therefore, may be more sensitive indicators of the people's apprehension regarding certain age crises.

4. European diseases such as smallpox, influenza, and measles seldom appear on bone either because the victim succumbs to the disease before the skeleton has a chance to respond or because recovery takes place too soon for bone involvement (Ortner 1979). The investigator must therefore rely on demographic structure, the incidence of nonspecific stress indicators such as periosteal reactions, and the spatial and stratigraphic disposition of mass graves to document the occurrence of European diseases in native American sites.

5. If male deaths at this age resulted from activities away from home and if these males were not transported back to the cemetery for interment, a similar ratio of male to female deaths during

the third decade might be observed. This possibility seems unlikely, however, given the nearly equal proportions of male and female adults in the sample.

6. The same results would obtain, irrespective of the way in which status was attained, if the subsistence economy provided nutrients sufficiently bountiful to ensure that members of both statuses enjoyed a protein-rich and balanced diet (see chapter 6).

3

Status, the Warrior Class, and Artificial Cranial Deformation

John Garrett

Artificial cranial deformation, the result of cradle-boarding or headbinding, is a phenomenon of long standing among native Americans (Stewart 1973; Ubelaker 1978). The remains of many residents of the King site exhibit purposeful deformation of the head, and it was a common practice at Etowah, Moundville in Alabama, and many other sites in the southeastern United States (Owsley and Guevin 1982).

The earliest reference to artificial cranial deformation appears to have been Hippocrates' description of the people of the Black Sea region. Attributing the peculiar form to "an artificial elongation of the head by compression during infancy," he stated that those who had the longest heads were considered the most noble (Wilson 1862). The earliest evidence of intentional cranial deformation occurs with the Shanidar 1 and 5 Neandertal skulls in Iraq, which date to at least forty-five thousand years ago. The appearance of this practice coincides with the earliest evidence of purposeful burial of the dead (Harrold 1980) and suggests a behavioral pattern associated with the development of *Homo sapiens* (Trinkaus 1982).

In the New World, intentional deformation of the head had become a widespread practice by the time of Christ (Stewart 1973). From Peru to the North American West Coast Columbia River people, to the Natchez and throughout the Mississippi River valley, to the people of Etowah and King, artificial cranial deformation is a visible reminder of a now largely obsolete cultural practice (Hrdlička 1905; Imbelloni 1950; Stewart 1950; Romero 1970).

Techniques used for cranial deformation differed from group to group, but most entailed binding the infant's head shortly after birth and continuing the pressure until the desired shape was formed. This usually took less than two years, but longer periods of binding have been observed (Ubelaker 1978). Neumann (1942) identified eight different types of artificial cranial deformation in the eastern United States. At the King site, deformation varied in the degree to which it was expressed, so it was not always possible to determine type, but parallelo-fronto-occipital seems to have been the most common (figure 3.1). This was accomplished by placing a board against the occiput and securing it to the head with a rope or cloth tied around the forehead. The board flattened the back of the head, while the rope or cloth produced a horizontal groove across the forehead. Often the resulting skull was larger when it was measured from side to side than when it was measured from front to back.

In the ethnographic literature, purposeful deformation of the head for aesthetic reasons is mentioned, but more often it is associated with tribal identity or the social organization of historic peoples (Hrdlička 1905; Owsley and Guevin 1982). The aptly

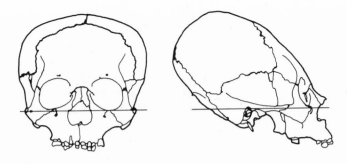

Figure 3.1
Front and lateral view
of a cranium with
parallelo-fronto-
occipital deformation.
After Neumann
1942:307. By
permission of the
publisher.

named Flathead Indians along the Columbia River used artificial cranial deformation as a badge of aristocratic descent (Wilson 1862:320–321). Early Peruvian Indians referred to their practice "as the custom of appearing fierce in war" (Wilson 1862:322). Although in both of these examples intentional deformation of the head was a societywide practice, others seem to have used it selectively to delineate segments within the larger population (Stewart 1973).

At the prehistoric Beaverdam Creek site in Georgia, for example, Blakely and Mathews (1985) found that artificial cranial deformation appeared only among females. They suggest that this sex-specific practice may have been for cosmetic purposes rather than to designate rank or descent. Only forty miles east of King at Etowah, deformation was divided almost equally between sexes but was more common in village-area remains than in Mound C remains (Blakely 1984). This distinction appears to be based on status, although temporal differences between the village-area and Mound C cemeteries complicate the picture (Larson 1971).

At the King site, one finds an equally complex situation. To check for intentional deformation, crania were reconstructed even if they were only partially preserved. Some skulls, crushed by earth pressure, were too badly distorted to evaluate for artificial deformation. This difficulty reduced the observable sample to sixty crania, of which only eight are undeformed. With 87 percent of the population exhibiting deformation, can artificial cranial deformation be correlated with status? And can one assume that King was a ranked society rather than an egalitarian one?

Status and rank in archaeologically defined societies can be inferred from mortuary treatment, iconographic depictions, and monumental architecture. On the assumption that individuals treated differently in life also will be treated differently in death (Binford 1971), most research on ranking has focused on mortuary practices (Saxe 1970; Brown 1971; Peebles 1974, 1977; Rothschild 1975; Tainter 1975; Hatch 1976; Blakely 1977; Seckinger 1977; Goldstein 1980). Since hierarchical societies normally include both hereditary and achieved ranks (Goldman 1970; Creamer and Haas 1985), mortuary ceremonialism should confirm the existence of two independent dimensions of social persona represented by the burials (see Peebles 1977; Peebles and Kus 1977). Inclusion of individuals in the superordinate dimension should be based on genealogical standing rather than on age and gender. In other words, burials should contain individuals of all ages and both genders and should exhibit symbols and evidence of extraordinary energy expenditure on mortuary ritual. Within the superordinate dimension, some infants and children will have the same rank as some adults and a higher rank than other adults.

At King, these criteria are met by interments in the public sector (figure 2.1). Public burials in the plaza and ceremonial structure contained men, women, and children and were commonly attended by rattlesnake and shell gorgets, copper-coated ear ornaments, caches of projectile points, and discoidals ("chunky stones").

The subordinate dimension, according to Peebles and Kus (1977), should be ordered on the basis of age, gender, and accomplishment. Generally, the older the individual, the greater the opportunity for achievement. Therefore, adult burials are typically more complex than juvenile burials; women are interred with some items not shared by men.

The subordinate dimension is present at King in the private sector. Grave goods, when present, commonly included Lamar and Dallas vessels, bone tools, shell beads, and mollusk shells. The dearth of rich grave accompaniments or high-status symbols and energy expenditure on mortuary treatment assign individuals interred in and around domestic structures to the low-status dimension (but see chapter 4). Within this dimension age and sex are correlated with mortuary variability, suggesting individually achieved ranks within the ascribed status. If this were the case, one could expect the burials in each category to decrease in number from bottom to top of the hierarchical scale, producing a pyramid of rank (Peebles 1977). Seckinger's (1977) analysis of grave accoutrements in both the public and private sectors of the site supports this hypothesis. It is clear, therefore, that King constituted a ranked society.

Occasionally, private sector burials held grave goods normally reserved for superordinate individuals. One burial in the private sector (Burial 92, a male in his mid-forties) contained the most conspicuous high-status grave goods recovered at the site (figure 3.2; Burial 57 in figure 3.3 held one projectile point and nine bone tools, grave goods more commonly associated with private sector males). Burial 92 included two iron celts and an iron spike of European origin, two copper plates, a stone-working kit, red ochre, 232 shell beads, and twenty-seven projectile points; Burial 92 also exhibited artificial cranial deformation.

Another intriguing private sector burial (Burial 49) involved a man in his forties. He did not exhibit cra-

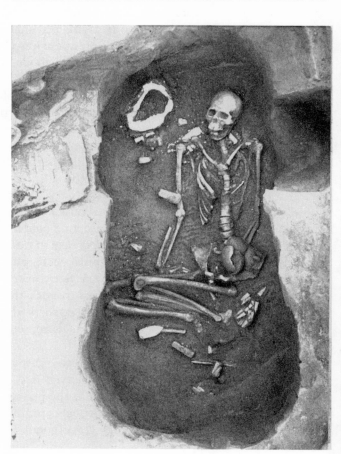

Figure 3.2
Burial 92 in situ, a private sector male in his forties, the most richly accompanied individual recovered at the King site

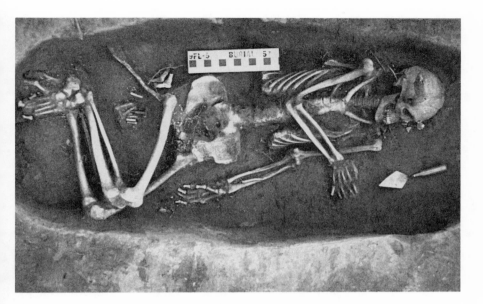

Figure 3.3
Burial 57 in situ, a private sector male in his twenties

nial deformation and yet was accompanied by an unusual number of grave goods, including a projectile point, some unworked stone, a blade, and a unique conch shell mask found located on the cranium. It is conceivable that the mask was intended to hide the undeformed head of an individual who, though born into low status, nevertheless achieved a superior rank. This initially suggested the possibility that artificial cranial deformation defined individuals who, under normal circumstances, were eligible for particular status or membership in certain classes. Modest support for this notion is drawn from the fact that private sector males with undeformed crania were typically among the burials containing the "poorest" or fewest grave goods. Unfortunately, the sample size was not large enough to permit statistical tests.

In the public sector, deformed crania were present in an 11 : 1 ratio—slightly higher than in the private sector. That these burials show both ascribed and achieved status is evident from the mixture of infants, children, and adults with different kinds and quantities of grave goods. Although a few females and children lacked grave associations, most were buried with some. All superordinate males were interred with grave accoutrements. Moreover, a number of these males were found with artifacts that seem associated with hunting and particularly with warfare, raising the possibility that there was a warrior class at King.

Larson (1972) notes that warfare or the threat of warfare was a regular feature of life in the southeastern United States at the time of the Spanish explorations. Virtually every polity encountered by Hernando de Soto in 1539–1542 was actively engaged either in forging alliances or in waging war with its neighbors (Garcilaso 1962; Elvas 1968). Archaeological evidence for warfare in the protohistoric Southeast includes bastioned palisades, dry moats, slave posts, skeletons exhibiting signs of scalping and penetrating wounds, trophy skulls, and grave goods suggestive of warrior status (Sears 1956; Larson 1972; Hally 1975a; Hudson 1976; Peebles 1983). Brown (1976) has convincingly argued that warfare was a prominent element in the iconography of the "Southern Cult."

The reasons for warfare in the Southeast seem to have been many. Gibson (1974) has proposed that in the lower Mississippi valley it served as a means of upward mobility in an otherwise rigidly ranked society. It is difficult to document this reason for warfare in the ethnohistoric and archaeological records, but indirect corroborative evidence may be the high status accorded accomplished warriors and the prominent display of war trophies (DePratter 1983). According to Hudson (1976), bravery in war, skill in craftsmanship, prowess in hunting, excellence in games, and success in healing were all criteria for achieving high rank in the Southeast.

Peebles (1983), citing ethnohistoric and archaeological evidence that hostilities often took the form of raids for slave labor, disrupting the productive activities of enemies, collecting tribute, and retaliatory strikes, has argued that warfare served principally the purpose of maintaining and defending boundaries and perpetuating large tracts of forest as buffer zones for deer hunting. Defense against attack is most evident in the fortifications surrounding villages and towns. Larson (1972) considers these defensive works to have been nearly impregnable. Attempts to breach the palisades would have been not only futile but extremely hazardous.

Larson (1972) suggests that perhaps the primary objective of warfare was the seizure and control of agricultural territory. What may be equally applicable to King is the view expressed by Caldwell (1958:64–65) that fortified towns were defenses against the intrusion of agricultural peoples into areas occupied by food-collecting groups. If Kestle (1984) is correct in saying that King was atypical in its reliance on gathering and hunting at a time of intensive crop domestication in the region, the implications are two: first, that maintenance of King's socioeconomic base (and that of the larger polity of which King was a part) required protection from invading agriculturalists and, second, that a warrior class was necessary to carry out these defensive measures.[1] As Kroeber (1963:148) has noted, a group that constantly shifts between war and peace is doomed to extinction.

Signs and symbols of indigenous, constant warfare at King include the palisade, the dry moat, the slave post, and the grave goods of both males and females.

Grave goods are most common among high-status public burials. Large caches of projectile points, stoneworking kits, flint blades and knives, bear penis bones, and red ochre were frequently found in high-status burials. Low-status burials contained grave goods consisting mostly of household and ornamental objects.

For historic Creeks red ochre symbolized the blood of enemies. Other southeastern Indians used it to enhance eyesight as well as to sharpen skills involved in rain making, lovemaking, and hunting (Hudson 1976:168–169). At King, red ochre was found associated only with exotic grave goods and likely indicates that these burials contained members of society held in high esteem. Stone projectile points embedded in bone or near distal skeletal elements and skulls showing signs of trauma may be evidence of warfare. Caches of anywhere from eight to fifty projectile points may reflect elite hunting and/or warrior status. The fact that all preserved male crania in the public sector exhibit artificial cranial deformation and were interred with warring accoutrements may indicate that there existed a select group whose warrior status was ascribed. However, this ascribed status did not preclude others from achieving high rank, even the rank of warrior class (see chapter 4).

Chi-square tests were performed to ascertain the likelihood of nonrandom associations between variables linked to mortuary activity. Two statistically significant associations were found: first, among cranially deformed adults, males were interred with grave goods more frequently than females (table 3.1); second, among deformed and undeformed adults, the probability that males rather than females would be buried with grave goods was significant beyond the .01 level (table 3.2). I conclude that status among females may have been derived from marriage to males. The absence of female children from the plaza and ceremonial structure would support the idea that women derived their status through marriage rather than by descent. Unfortunately, the sex of subadolescent skeletons cannot be determined because secondary sex traits do not develop until puberty; and the grave associations, in this instance, offer no clues.

In conclusion, whatever their intentions, the King site people seem to have been inextricably bound to warfare. War with neighboring Indians was eventually replaced by war with Europeans, but the conflicts remained essentially the same. As Garcilaso de la Vega observed, "A cacique [chief] does not carry on warfare with just one of his neighbors, but with all who share his boundaries, for whether there be two, three, four or more, all wage war upon each other—a

Table 3.1 Chi-square test of the association between grave goods and sex among cranially deformed adults

	Artifacts	No artifacts	N
Males	17	9	26
Females	8	18	26
Total	25	27	52

Note: $\chi^2 = 4.462$, $p = .02$; significant.

Table 3.2 Chi-square test of the association between grave goods and sex within the total adult population

	Artifacts	No artifacts	N
Males	28	10	38
Females	18	37	55
Total	46	47	93

Note: $\chi^2 = 15.059$, $p < .01$; significant.

for no one becomes careless and each can demonstrate his individual gallantry" (Varner and Varner 1951:489). Warfare is reflected in the King site fortification and by the remnants of war left in the mortuary patterning. The survival of the King site residents—at least until shortly after the Spanish arrival—depended upon a well-delineated warrior class whose members both earned and occasionally inherited their status.

The correlation between artificial cranial deformation and status admittedly remains problematic and deserves further study. But the evidence cited herein clearly demonstrates the extent to which the King site occupants were tied both symbolically and actually to warfare. The association between the cultural practice of intentional deformation of the head, social organization, and warfare needs to be examined at other sites in the Southeast in order to develop models of biocultural adaptation that will help us to test both intrasite regularities and intersite interactions.

Notes

1. *Editor's note:* Not all communities in the Coosa chiefdom were as well fortified as King. Defensive perimeters seem to have been absent at central towns such as the Little Egypt site (Hally 1979), which Hudson et al. (*Chiefdom,* 1985, 1987) have identified as the capital of the chiefdom. That they were present at frontier villages such as King suggests that outlying communities served as the first line of defense against "outside" marauders, while warfare was uncommon near the center of the chiefdom. In any event, the need for warriors at King has been well established.

John Garrett

4

**Cultural
Affiliations of
the King Site**

Lisa E. Crowder

Attempts to place the King site in a regional cultural context have linked the site with the Dallas and Mouse Creek groups, two contemporaneous groups from Tennessee (Garrow and Smith 1973; Hally 1975b; Garrow 1975; Seckinger 1975). I shall focus here on burial practices and architecture, and also briefly on settlement plan, to probe the relationship between King and the Dallas and Mouse Creek cultures and between King and the people of the Middle Cumberland region of Tennessee.

Dallas, Mouse Creek, and Middle Cumberland

The terms "Dallas," "Mouse Creek," and "Middle Cumberland" refer to cultures known from the archaeological record. The Dallas culture, which is widely held to be ancestral to the historic native American group known collectively as the Creek, occupied a large territory in the Southeast from about A.D. 1250 to 1600. This territory, the Great

Valley region of Tennessee, is an intermontane depression in eastern Tennessee and western Georgia drained by the Tennessee and Coosa River systems. According to Lewis and Kneberg (1946:10), the Dallas culture is distinguished by its use of "substructure mounds; community buildings and dwellings constructed of large logs; burials (predominantly partly flexed) interred in village areas and substructure mounds;" and shell gorgets and other characteristics relating to the ceramic and stone industries.

The political system of the Dallas people was highly complex, with a great number of small, rural towns being subject to large ceremonial centers. The relatively few large centers, the political and economic hubs of Dallas society, have provided the bulk of our knowledge about the Dallas culture (Hatch 1976). However, life in these ceremonial centers (Dallas, Hiwassee Island, and Etowah) was not typical of life for all the members of the Dallas culture. The majority of the people lived in the rural towns. The Mouse Creek people seem to represent such a group.

Mouse Creek refers to an East Tennessee group that occupied the region between the North and South Mouse Creeks and surrounding areas between A.D. 1500 and 1650. The Mouse Creek culture is similar to Dallas, although it does exhibit several characteristic differences (figure 4.1). Mounds are not commonly associated with the Mouse Creek sites, although the reason may be the brief occupation of the Mouse Creek sites and their small size rather than any basic difference in the belief systems of the two groups.

The architecture of the Mouse Creek people is one of the factors used to differentiate between the Dallas and Mouse Creek groups. While the floors of

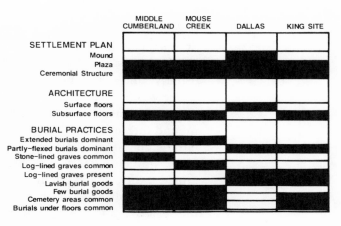

Figure 4.1
Middle Cumberland, Mouse Creek, Dallas, and King site settlement plans, architecture, and burial practices

Dallas structures were level with the outside surface, the floors of Mouse Creek structures were usually twelve to eighteen inches below the ground outside the structure. The settlement plans of the two groups are very similar, with the towns of both having domestic structures clustered around a central plaza. Mounds with ceremonial structures are found in the Dallas public areas and, while mounds are not commonly associated with Mouse Creek settlements, large public buildings are usually found in the plaza area (Lewis and Kneberg 1955).

It is in the area of burial practices that the greatest difference is found between the Dallas and Mouse Creek peoples. When a person in a Dallas town died, the body was placed in a semiflexed position in a grave. The graves were not usually prepared after being dug to fit the corpse. Occasionally, the bodies appear to have been wrapped in a coarse textile or twilled-plaited matting (Lewis and Kneberg 1946). Single interments are the general rule with Dallas burials. The burials were typically located in the plaza directly bordering on the domestic structures or, for individuals who had attained a higher status in life, in the substructure mound. Burials are not usually under the house floors in Dallas towns. There was a high degree of differentiation in the frequency of burial goods between the plaza and mound interments at Dallas sites. While most plaza burials contained little more than pottery or a few stone implements, the mound burials often contained exotic goods such as paraphernalia of the Southern Cult, iron implements, exotic goods from the seacoast, and other items that the Dallas people would have regarded as rare (Hatch 1976).

The burials of the Mouse Creek people were not as lavish as those of the Dallas people. A large number of Mouse Creek burials contained no grave goods, and the richest of the burials did not rival those of the Dallas mound burials. At Mouse Creek sites people are often buried under house floors. Similarly, two and sometimes more bodies were in many cases placed directly on top of one another in a single grave. Mouse Creek people were most commonly buried in a fully extended position. Log or stone slab tombs are common. Mouse Creek is also distinctive in that certain areas of the town were apparently designated as cemeteries. Typically in certain areas large numbers of burials are clustered, often with one or more burials intruding on another (Lewis and Kneberg 1955).

As Lewis and Kneberg (1955) noted, the Mouse Creek culture (A.D. 1500–1650) is very similar to that of the Middle Cumberland people of Tennessee. In the area of burial practices the similarity of the Mouse Creek and Middle Cumberland peoples is most apparent. The Middle Cumberland people are known as the "Stone Grave people" because they

Lisa E. Crowder

buried their dead in stone-lined graves. Members of this culture were placed in their graves in a fully extended position with even the fingers and toes extended. Mouse Creek burials also exhibit this full extension although, because eastern Tennessee does not have as much limestone as the Cumberland Valley area, stone-lined graves are not found at Mouse Creek sites as often as at Middle Cumberland sites. Log-lined tombs are, however, fairly common among the Mouse Creek peoples (Lewis and Kneberg 1955).

Both the Mouse Creek and Middle Cumberland peoples placed large numbers of graves in certain areas of their towns. These cemetery areas are clusterings of graves rather than mass graves, although burials of several people together are fairly common among both groups. Mouse Creek and Middle Cumberland burials are also similar in the type and quantity of grave goods left with the dead. Few grave goods are associated with burials in either Mouse Creek or Middle Cumberland sites.

There is evidence that burials beneath houses occur at Middle Cumberland sites[1] and that structures with subsurface floors are not uncommon.[2] If these characteristics prove to be typical of the culture as a whole, then we would have further evidence linking the Middle Cumberland and Mouse Creek peoples. One other factor that may link the two groups is time. The Mouse Creek phase began around the time of European contact and was of a relatively short duration. The Middle Cumberland peoples lived in the Nashville area during the Mississippian period for centuries; however, no European artifacts are found with Middle Cumberland burials. Lewis and Kneberg (1955) proposed a theory of mass migration to explain the similarities between Middle Cumberland and Mouse Creek cultures, a theory at least partially corroborated by Berryman (1980) in his study of crania from Middle Cumberland, Mouse Creek, and Dallas sites.

According to Berryman's analysis (1980:7), the crania of Dallas and Middle Cumberland males differ significantly at the .025 level, and Dallas and Middle Cumberland females differ at the .01 level. In contrast, there is no significant difference between males or females of the Middle Cumberland and Mouse Creek groups. Although Dallas and Mouse Creek males exhibited no significant difference, Dallas and Mouse Creek females did differ significantly at the .025 level (figure 4.2). The results suggest that the Middle Cumberland and Mouse Creek samples were drawn from the same population. Furthermore, the Middle Cumberland group exhibits greater biological distance from the Dallas sample than does the Mouse Creek group.[3] Thus— to the degree that phenotypic skeletal attributes can be correlated with archaeologically defined cultural groups—Berryman's findings can be used to support the theory that the Mouse Creek people represent a migration of Middle Cumberland people into eastern Tennessee.

Figure 4.2
Diagrammatic representation of the relative distinctiveness of male and female crania from Dallas, Mouse Creek, and Middle Cumberland

Lisa E. Crowder

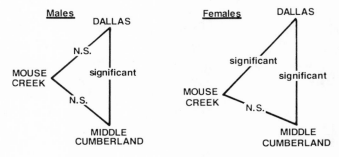

Using this information as a base, let us now examine the King site. As mentioned above, the King site has been linked with both the Mouse Creek and Dallas cultures (Garrow and Smith 1973; Garrow 1975; Hally 1975b; Seckinger 1975). If we proceed on the assumption that Dallas and Mouse Creek people are merely different elements of the same culture—urban and rural variants, respectively—then it is not difficult to explain the presence of both elements at the King site. If, on the other hand, we accept the Lewis and Kneberg theory that the Mouse Creek people represent a Middle Cumberland migration into Dallas territory, then we must explain why King exhibits characteristics of both groups. In this chapter I explore the latter hypothesis.

When the King site culture is examined in its component parts—architecture, settlement pattern, and burial practices—and is compared with Dallas and Mouse Creek, certain inconsistencies arise. Architecturally the site is virtually indistinguishable from Mouse Creek sites (figure 4.1). Structures exhibit subsurface floors that were excavated to an average depth of approximately twelve to eighteen inches, and the entrance ways of the structures were of the exterior-vestibule type associated with the Mouse Creek phase. The settlement plan of the site is also of the Mouse Creek type, with an open plaza, no substructure mound, large public buildings, and a palisade and dry moat surrounding the town. As stated previously, settlement plans do not differ significantly between Dallas and Mouse Creek sites.

In the area of burial practices, the King site people exhibited elements characteristic of both the Dallas and Mouse Creek cultures. The vast majority of the King site people were buried in a semiflexed position

(Dallas), and while single interments were in the majority, multiple interments were found at the King site (Mouse Creek). All of the individuals buried in the public structure were in an extended position (Mouse Creek), and most showed evidence of having been buried in log tombs (Mouse Creek). In type and quantity, the goods found in the burials more closely resembled those found at Dallas sites, being more lavish in nature than those typically found in Mouse Creek or Middle Cumberland sites (Hatch 1976). Many burials were found under the floors of domestic structures, and some areas of the town appear to have been set aside as cemeteries (Mouse Creek).

As is evident, the King site can be placed firmly in neither the Dallas nor the Mouse Creek culture, for while the site appears to be most closely affiliated with Mouse Creek, several attributes associated with the Dallas culture are present.

Discussion

Assuming with Lewis and Kneberg that a Middle Cumberland migration into Dallas territory occurred, and further assuming that the people of the Dallas culture were ancestors of the Creek people of historic times, we can make an educated guess as to why the King site exhibits elements of both groups. The Creek Indians traditionally incorporated other tribes into their group. In fact, the Creek people were known as a confederacy of peoples from the earliest recorded descriptions. Small tribes and groups that had been forced from their traditional lands by other, hostile Indians joined the Creek and created a large, diverse, and powerful group. While all of the Creek peoples exhibited certain characteristics in common, there was still a degree of variation within the confederacy, and each town was self-sufficient (Swanton 1928). The Yuchi, one group incorporated into the confederacy, did not even speak a Muskogean language and remained quite distinct within the confederacy.

Taking this diversity into account, we may speculate that the Mouse Creek people do indeed represent Middle Cumberland people being incorporated into the Dallas (Creek) culture. As the Middle Cumberland people moved into Dallas territory, they began to be drawn into the Dallas culture politically, socially, and materially.

Creek Social Organization

The historic Creek people had a highly complex social organization. Towns within the chiefdom were either "white" or "red." In southeastern Indian symbolism, white is the color of peace, unity, and that which is established and old. Red is the color of disunity, unfamiliarity, and war (Hudson 1976). It seems likely that peoples newly incorporated into the confederacy were under suspicion, and therefore their towns were regarded as red towns, or areas of possible conflict. Perhaps as time went on, and the people became established within the confederacy through ties of kinship and economics, their town's status changed.

The Creek red and white divisions also existed within their kinship structure. The people of the two divisions were called either the "Hathagalgi," or "white people" (also called "those who stick together"), and the "Tcilokogalgi," or "people of different speech" (Hudson 1976:236). When we take into account the kinship structure of southeastern Indians—exogamous, matrilineal clans—we can hypothesize that the terms "Hathagalgi" and "Tcilokogalgi" arose to differentiate between the older, established clans and the clans of the newly incorporated peoples. In this case it would be very natural to generically label all newcomers "people of different speech" instead of giving each new group a different label.

Within the clans, there was also a hierarchy of social status. Certain clans were considered higher than others—particularly white clans such as the Wind and Bear clans—and those born to them were more likely to be appointed to high positions. According to Hudson (1976), the southeastern Indians "ranked themselves partly with respect to age and partly with respect to their accomplishments as warriors, leaders of men, and as religious and medical practitioners" (p. 203). Although the southeastern groups were matrilineal, women rarely achieved power within the group.

The King site contains evidence of internal status stratification that follows location of burials within the town. While most burials were located in the domestic zone within and around the dwellings of the people, other burials were located in the public plaza and the large ceremonial structure at the northern end of the plaza. Previous investigators (Hally 1975b; Seckinger 1975; Garrett 1984) have concluded that individuals buried within the public areas—the plaza and ceremonial structure—held higher status in life than the average member of the society. Moreover, since men, women, and children are represented in this burial sample, it appears that their status was ascriptive, or hereditary.

The Creek, as mentioned above, recognized certain clans as being of a higher status than others, and therefore people born to these clans automatically enjoyed a higher status. It is possible that, at the King site, burial in the public sector was considered a birthright of the more important clan(s). However, within Creek society the way to gain true status was through deeds. Achieved status, through acts of bravery in war, medical prowess, or excellence in chunky, was far more meaningful than the ascriptive status of the clan (Hudson 1976).

The situation seems to have been similar at the King site. The treatment of the dead suggests that the King site people valued certain members of their society more than even those buried in the public sector. While those individuals buried within the ceremonial structure were given adequate burials, they are by no means the most lavish within the site. The two finest burials within the ceremonial structure are Burial 105, a male in his mid-forties, which contained fifty projectile points, and Burial 101, a man about fifty, which contained seven points, stoneworking tools, two discoidals, and a large blade. But private sector Burial 92 is by far the richest at the site (figure 3.2). This log tomb burial of a man in his forties contained red ochre, a stoneworking kit, a blade, 232 beads, twenty-seven stone projectile points, two copper plates, a conch shell, two iron celts, and one iron spike. Another lavish interment, Burial 117, is located on the periphery of the public sector, seemingly belonging to neither the public nor the private sector. This burial of a young adult of indeterminate (male?) sex contained red ochre, a stoneworking kit, a spatulate axe, an iron celt, a chunky stone, an iron knife, and worked bone. Contained within these two burials (92 and 117) are five of the eight iron implements found in the entire site. This iron could have come only from contact with Europeans and was therefore extremely rare. For the goods to have been buried with these people indicates that they were of very high status. That such lavish burials occur within the private, or domestic, sector would seem to confirm that achieved status held more value than ascriptive status for the King site people, just as it did for the Creek.

The King site, then, represents a population of Middle Cumberland/Mouse Creek in the process of acculturation into the Dallas/Creek culture. As the two groups became more closely involved, the belief systems of each began to be affected. The change from an extended position to a semiflexed position in burials of the dead indicates that some shift in beliefs occurred between the time that the groups arrived at the Mouse Creek area and the time that the King site was inhabited. Also, the more lavish goods buried with the dead would seem to indicate not only a change in beliefs but a greater surplus economy. As time went by, the people who had once been the Middle Cumberland people perhaps became more important in the redistributive system of the Dallas people. Through time the merging of the groups undoubtedly became greater and greater until finally, beginning in the eighteenth century, the confederacy of Creek people came to be documented in detail by William Bartram, James Adair, Benjamin Hawkins, and, in the twentieth century, John Swanton.

Conclusions

In this chapter I have shown that the inhabitants of the King site likely represent the descendants of the Middle Cumberland people of the Cumberland Valley area of Tennessee in the process of incorporation into the Dallas culture of eastern Tennessee. The Mouse Creek people represent the same basic group as the King site inhabitants but in a slightly less acculturated state. I further believe that the Dallas people are indeed ancestral to the historic Upper Creek tribes and that the incorporation of the people of the Middle Cumberland, Mouse Creek, and King sites into the Dallas culture merely represents an early example of the adding of a group to the confederacy of tribes that is well documented in later times.

More research is necessary to substantiate these hypotheses. This additional research could focus on tracking specific elements such as the use of stone box graves, the frequency of burial position, the use of subsurface floors, and other elements that are most variable within the homogeneous Mississippian period in the region.

Notes

1. Stone box graves were located under the floors of domestic structures at the Ganier site on the Cumberland River (Broster 1972).

2. The structures located at the Arnold site near the Little Harpeth River exhibited subsurface floors which the investigator of the site described as "large saucer-shaped depressions" (Ferguson 1972).

3. *Editor's note:* "Biological distance" is a statistical expression of the total morphological difference between population samples. The multivariate analysis, using either discrete nonmetric traits or measurements, weighs the variables from all individuals comprising each sample to arrive at an overall measure of intergroup distinctiveness; at the same time, it provides an index of intragroup homogeneity or heterogeneity. Generally, the greater the within-groups homogeneity, the greater the between-groups distance (Blackith and Reyment 1971). Therefore, it can be used not only to describe the genetic distance between samples—to the extent that the variables have a hereditary component—but also to suggest the degree of inbreeding within a population or the amount of interbreeding (often exogamy) between populations.

II

Stress, Diet, and Disease

5

**Subsistence
and Sex Roles**

Sharon Kestle

Tooth wear and caries are sensitive indicators of sub-sistence and dietary practices (Armelagos 1969; Smith 1972; Buikstra and Cook 1980; Smith, Bar-Yosef, and Sillen 1984). Dental attrition at the King site was analyzed to determine dietary patterns and to assess sexual division of labor in the acquisition of food. One purpose was to test Larsen's (1982) hy-pothesis that differential wear between the sexes often reflects male/female food procurement roles and sex-specific uses of the teeth as tools. I studied dental attrition between the anterior and posterior teeth of King site males and females and overall wear in both sexes. I developed a quantitative scale to assess the attrition of all observable dentitions from the site. The results indicate that King's resi-dents had a largely foraging subsistence economy. Greater attrition among females suggests that women played a more important role in limited agri-cultural production.

Carious teeth were also observed as an indicator of dietary/subsistence patterns. As a rule, corn agriculturalists exhibit more caries than gathering/hunting groups because bacteria in the mouth convert the sucrose in corn to acid that destroys the enamel and dentin of teeth (Molnar 1971; Cassidy 1972; Larsen 1984; Perzigian, Tench, and Braun 1984), and the "sticky" consistency of porridges made from corn thwarts attempts to clean the teeth (Cook 1984; Powell 1985). Since the incidence of caries covaries with the amount of corn consumed, caries can be used to suggest the relative proportion of maize in diets (Rose et al. 1984). In general, frequencies of caries among native Americans range from 0 to 10 percent for gatherers and hunters and from 8 to 25 percent for food producers (Turner 1979; Cohen and Armelagos 1984; Powell 1985).

Substantially fewer caries were found in the King remains than in the Etowah remains, which represent a roughly contemporaneous and largely agricultural population located some forty miles east of the King site (Kelly and Larson 1957; Blakely and Beck 1981). Trace element analysis was used to corroborate dental findings as they relate to the subsistence of King's people. Although trace element analysis has its detractors (Elias 1980), anthropologists have successfully used trace element data from archaeological samples to deduce dietary stress (Gilbert 1977, 1985; Sillen 1981; Price and Kavanagh 1982; Schoeninger 1982; Sillen and Kavanagh 1982). The analysis appears particularly useful for identifying the gross dietary differences that normally exist between foragers and agriculturalists (Gilbert 1975).

Materials and Methods

Fifty-five King site individuals in toto were used in this study. Subadults with deciduous teeth or incompletely erupted permanent teeth were excluded, so that the sample ranged in age from the late teens to nearly eighty years. Using the Smirnov test, and the .05 level of confidence, no statistically significant differences were found between the age structures of males and females. In this way I controlled for age in comparisons of attrition and incidences of caries between the sexes (although there were slightly more older males than older females).

To assess wear, I first divided the dentition into four quadrants: upper left, upper right, lower left, and lower right. Only two quadrants—one upper and one lower—from each individual were selected for analysis in order to reduce the effects of antemortem tooth loss on wear. The teeth for the quadrants chosen were then divided into two sections, an anterior section, incisors and canines, and a posterior section, premolars and molars. Wear on each tooth was scored by assigning to it a numerical value corresponding to a scale of attrition that ranged from zero (no wear) to four (very pronounced wear).[1] The average wear for the anterior and posterior dentition was calculated by summing the numerical scores for all teeth and dividing the total by the number of teeth in each section. A similar procedure was followed to determine average wear for the entire quadrant.

As previously mentioned, comparisons of the percentages of caries were made between the King sample and Etowah village sample to see how closely tooth decay at King matched that of a population reliant on cultigens. It should be noted that nuts and mollusks also appear to have been staples of the diet at Etowah (Blakely and Beck 1981; Beck 1985). Percentages of caries for each individual were obtained by dividing the total number of carious teeth by the total number of teeth present in the anterior and posterior portions of the dental arch. Since the incidence of caries is age progressive, I also compared frequencies within and between samples using the age categories seventeen to thirty years, thirty-one to forty-five years, and forty-six years and older. Finally, I compared the incidence of caries between males and females from the King and Etowah sites.

Brown and Blakely (1985) analyzed distributions of trace elements at the King site. Levels of calcium, copper, magnesium, strontium, and zinc were assayed by means of atomic emission spectroscopy using an inductively coupled plasma optical emission spectrometer (Boumans 1978). These elements were chosen because they are thought to be reasonably reliable indicators of certain dietary intakes and stresses (Price and Kavanagh 1982; Sillen and Kavanagh 1982; Gilbert 1985). Zinc and copper, for example, are found predominantly in meats and seafoods, whereas strontium and magnesium are more commonly obtained through whole grains and cereals (Underwood 1977). Strontium also occurs in high concentrations in nuts and shellfish (Gilbert 1977). The analysis used samples of five to ten grams of cortical bone removed from the shafts of well-preserved femurs. (See Szpunar, Lambert, and Buikstra 1978 and Brown and Blakely 1985 for procedures.) These data were helpful in determining the general food classes consumed by the King site inhabitants. This in turn could suggest the sources of cariogenesis as well as foodstuffs contributing to wear (Gilbert 1985). The amounts of zinc and strontium at the King site were compared with elemental levels at the Dallas site in Tennessee to determine the difference in diets between the nearly contemporaneous populations (Geidel 1982; Hatch and Geidel 1983).

Diagenesis at the two sites, or postmortem changes in the chemical composition of bone due to soil conditions or mortuary practices (see Gordon and Buikstra 1981), appears to have been minimal (Geidel 1982; Brown and Blakely 1985). Differences in trace element concentrations obviously cannot be attributed to diet or disease when they are actually the result of diagenesis. At the King site, diagenesis was negligible for the following reasons.

1. The short occupation of the town ensures that all skeletons had been in the ground for nearly the same length of time.
2. There are no mound burials.
3. All interments are primary inhumations.
4. Although preservation is variable, it does not seem to have affected remains in various parts of the site differently.
5. All skeletons are found above the water table.
6. The pH level at the site today is above 5.0, suggesting that the soil was not so acidic as to dissolve bone and release trace elements to be carried off by ground water. However, the occasional use of lime by modern farmers in the region may have slightly elevated the pH from its aboriginal level.

Results and Discussion

Tooth wear varies greatly from one native American skeletal population to another (Powell 1985). As Molnar (1971) tells us, "Often the degree and kinds of tooth wear vary from population to population. This variability is possibly related to certain material aspects of culture such as diet, food preparation techniques and tool usage" (p. 104). The difference between anterior and posterior tooth wear among inhabitants of the King site was considerable, with anterior wear being much more pronounced than posterior wear. On the scale of zero to four, from least to greatest wear, the anterior dentition for the total sample (sexes combined) averaged 3.4 and the posterior dentition averaged 2.6. One would expect anterior wear to exceed posterior wear, since the front teeth erupt at an earlier age than all but one of the back teeth, but the difference is greater than can be accounted for by the eruption schedule alone.

The excessive anterior wear can be explained in at least two ways. First, the King site occupants may have been somewhat less agricultural than was previously thought. According to Hinton (1981), "Those people pursuing a hunting and gathering subsistence strategy routinely exhibit appreciably greater wear in the anterior portion of the dental arches than do those associated with a food-producing economy with somewhat the opposite tendency" (p. 556). Second, the King site inhabitants may have been using the anterior teeth as tools (Blakely and Beck 1984). Concerning the use of teeth as tools, Brose (1972) has noted that "the use of teeth as tools can involve any of the teeth, although there is some indication that the anterior teeth may be more often employed" (p. 517). Of course, these two possibilities are not mutually exclusive.

The values obtained for anterior tooth wear between King site males and females are 3.7 and 3.1, respectively; using a chi-square test corrected for continuity, the difference proved statistically significant (table 5.1). The posterior wear is nearly the same for males and females. The greater amount of anterior wear in males may reflect sex-specific differences in diet, perhaps related to food procurement—male hunting versus female plant collecting—or sex-specific uses of the teeth as tools. The practices among Australian aborigines of finishing the edges of stone projectile points by pressure flaking with the teeth (Gould 1968) and holding needles

Table 5.1 Anterior and posterior tooth wear between males and females at the King site

	Wear values below 3.0	Wear values above 3.0	N
Anterior wear[a]			
Males	3	23	26
Females	10	19	29
Total	13	42	55
Posterior wear[b]			
Males	18	8	26
Females	23	6	29
Total	41	14	55

[a]$\chi^2 = 3.884$, $p < .05$; significant. [b]$\chi^2 = .754$, $p > .05$; not significant.

and biting threads (Schour and Sarnat 1942) produce different degrees of attrition and different patterns of attrition.

Hinton (1981) reports that, "while dietary abrasiveness may be a primary determinant of the degree and rate of wear, the forms of wear are chiefly a reflection of the patterns of functional jaw movement and tooth use" (p. 556). Furthermore, the morphology of an individual's dental arcade and shape of the teeth may be partly responsible for the type of wear displayed. Hinton (1981) observes: "Differences in tooth size, shape and arch position may also influence forms and rate of wear; it is likely that the nature of tooth use plays a major role in shaping the form of wear on the anterior teeth" (p. 557). Sex differences in anterior wear at King almost surely stem from a sexual division of labor, but the data fail to show whether the differences are due to diet or to use of the teeth as tools.

On average, 17 percent of the teeth per individual at Etowah were carious, as compared with 12 percent per individual at King (figure 5.1). Again, the explanation is that the two populations had different diets and therefore different subsistence patterns. Since agriculturalists typically display more caries than gathering/hunting groups, we may infer that King was less agricultural than Etowah.

I next compared the frequencies of caries between males and females in the Etowah and King samples. The Smirnov test indicated that differences in the age structures at the two sites were not statistically significant. At Etowah, males and females had almost the same percentages of caries, males being 15 percent and females 18 percent. In the King sample there were far more caries among females—16 percent to males' 8 percent—a difference that, according to a chi-square test corrected for continuity, is statistically significant. This result suggests a difference in diet between men and women. Such a difference has been observed in gathering and hunting societies elsewhere. Molnar (1971) states, "This

Figure 5.1
Seventeen percent of the Etowah teeth per individual ($N = 65$) are carious, compared with 12 percent of the King teeth per individual ($N = 59$).

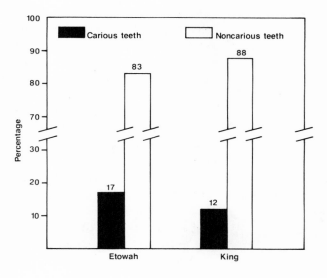

would suggest that there is a contrast between male and female activities in hunting and gathering cultures which does not exist at the agricultural level" (p. 187).

Frequencies of carious teeth at King and Etowah were also compared between age groups of seventeen to thirty years, thirty-one to forty-five years, and forty-six years and older. After I controlled for antemortem tooth loss, the figures at King were 8 percent, 23 percent, and 19 percent, respectively. So there is a substantially higher incidence of carious teeth in the thirty-one-to-forty-five age category than in the younger and older groups for both samples. This apparent paradox has three possible explanations: (1) periodontal disease, which if severe enough could cause death—mainly by blood poisoning—at an early age, so that the affected individuals would not be represented in the older sample; (2) a new group of people moved onto the site; (3) a change in subsistence took place at the village. Given the lack of genetic diversity in the two burial populations (Corruccini 1974; Crowder 1985) and the constancy through time of trace element levels and cortical bone thickness at the two sites (Blakely and Beck 1981; Brown and Blakely 1985; Blakely and Brown 1985), the first explanation is the most plausible.

Trace element analysis of the King remains by Brown and Blakely (1985) yields further information about the subsistence pattern. Magnesium, strontium, and zinc were found in high concentrations among both males and females, indicating a diet high in meat, nuts, and whole grains and cereals. In comparison with the Dallas site in Tennessee, King is particularly high in strontium and zinc, suggesting that the King people consumed more wild plant foods, while the Dallas occupants ate more domestic plant foods (Geidel 1982; Hatch and Geidel 1983). Taken together, the data clearly demonstrate that King's inhabitants foraged more than some late prehistoric and protohistoric groups in the region.

In summary, it has been shown by Larsen (1982) that agricultural peoples on the Georgia coast experienced more tooth wear and higher frequencies of caries than the nonagricultural peoples. Therefore, the small amount of wear and decay at the King site in comparison with Etowah indicates a subsistence economy less dependent on food production than food collection. That the incidence of caries among females is twice that of males at King supports the idea that men and women were consuming somewhat different foodstuffs and may reflect a sexual division of labor in food procurement. However, this hypothesis is not strongly supported by the trace element tests. The amount of dental wear between males and females is also markedly different, with the anterior portion of the dentition being significantly more worn among males. Thus men were using the anterior teeth in ways different from females and possibly as tools. Detailed studies now under way on the teeth of King's residents, including analyses of enamel chippage and enamel hypoplasias in conjunction with attrition and cavitation, may shed light on questions raised in this chapter.

Notes

1. The numerical scale was as follows: 0 = absent, 1 = slight (enamel polished), 2 = moderate (dentin partially exposed), 3 = pronounced (dentin entirely exposed), 4 = very pronounced (pulp or pulp and roots exposed).

6

Diet and
Nutritional Stress

Antoinette B. Brown

King site individuals were assigned after death to one of two distinct burial areas: a private area or a public one (see figure 2.1). The presence of public burials in the center of the village and the distribution of exotic grave goods suggest that public burials represent individuals of a higher status than those in the private burials. Since young children, who would have had no opportunity to earn status, are found among the high-status burials, it is probable that status at the King site could be ascribed as well as attained.

Ascribed status is one of the characteristics of a chiefdom level of sociopolitical organization as described by Service (1962). Peebles and Kus (1977) have indicated some of the archaeological correlates of ranked societies. Hatch and Willey (1974) analyzed the skeletal remains from Dallas culture burials in eastern Tennessee to identify a relationship between status and stature as a derivative feature of the Service model.

Status was manifest in mortuary artifacts in the Dallas sample. Both qualitative and quantitative differences between status categories covaried with burial age, sex, and location within the site. With regard to stature, a statistically significant difference exists in average stature between artifactually defined high- and low-status males but not between high- and low-status females. Status differences are therefore apparently reflected in the stature of artifactually defined high-status males, but a similar pattern cannot be demonstrated for females (Hatch and Willey 1974).

A statistically significant difference in mean stature also exists between locational categories for males but not for females. The mean stature of males found in mound burials is greater than that of males found in village burials. The stature difference among females is not significant (Hatch and Willey 1974). Differences between the high- and low-status groups in nutrition, genetic makeup, and disease history were suggested as possible origins of the stature differences.

The King site skeletons were analyzed for adult stature with the hypothesis that the public and private burials would show differences in mean stature. But using formulas developed for native Americans by Neumann and Waldman (1968), it was found that males in both the public and the private areas attained a mean height of 168 cm (5 feet, 6 inches) and females in both the public and the private areas averaged 157 cm (5 feet, 2 inches). Since the hypothesis was not supported by the data, an alternative was sought. The new hypothesis was that at the King site the inhabitants did not experience deficiencies in dietary resources that would lead to resource rationing on the basis of status. This hypothesis is consistent with the skeletal evidence. The analysis of trace elements indicates a mixed diet with no elemental differences between the public and private burials (Brown and Blakely 1985). Furthermore, there is a relatively low incidence of dental disease compared with that in agriculturally dependent populations that consumed large amounts of corn (Kestle 1984). To test this hypothesis, data regarding cortical bone thickness were obtained through radiographs of well-preserved femurs and tibias. Relatively thick cortexes reflect adequate resources, while thinner cortexes reflect inadequate calorie and protein resources.

The Nature of Cortical Change

The cortical bone is the compact bone between the outer surface and the marrow, or medullary, cavity. The subperiosteal part of a tubular bone is the outer surface of the cortex; the endosteal part of the bone is the inner surface of the cortex next to the medullary cavity. Bone deposit is termed "apposition"; bone loss is termed "resorption." If, hypothetically, subperiosteal apposition and endosteal resorption were occurring at equal rates, then the diameter of both the bone and the medullary cavity would be increasing while the thickness of the cortex remained unchanged.

A radiograph of a tubular bone in a sufficiently standardized projection reveals the subperiosteal surfaces and the medullary cavity, which may then be measured as the total subperiosteal diameter (T) and the medullary cavity width (M), as illustrated in figure 6.1. Such measurements are highly replicable on a single radiograph, on a set of radiographs, and over long periods of time (Garn 1970). By subtracting

M from T, we may calculate cortical thickness (C), and the final replicability of C approximates that of T and M.

T corresponds to the total subperiosteal diameter, and increases in T measure linear subperiosteal apposition, or gain. M corresponds to the medullary cavity width, and changes in M reflect endosteal resorption or endosteal apposition (Garn 1970). C, that is ($T - M$), corresponds to the summed medial and lateral wall thicknesses. Changes in C may reflect increases in T or increases or decreases in M.

If C is taken as a percentage of T, either as a linear measurement or as a set of areas, then a new set of data is disclosed, as illustrated in figure 6.2. The ratio of C to T is a simple measure of bone density. Expressed as an area (in square millimeters), if the area of C is 50 percent of the area of T, then the bone section in question has exactly half the physical density of a solid cylinder of the same diameter T.

T increases throughout life. M at first increases in childhood and then decreases from puberty to the

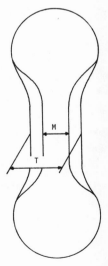

Figure 6.1
Diagrammatic representation of tubular bone, showing midshaft measurements of T and M. Adapted from Garn 1970:4. Courtesy of Charles C Thomas, Publisher, Springfield, Illinois.

Figure 6.2
Representations of
total subperiosteal
area, medullary area,
and cortical area as
derived from *T* and *M*.
Adapted from Garn
1970:11. Courtesy of
Charles C Thomas,
Publisher, Springfield,
Illinois.

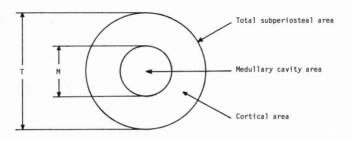

Figure 6.2 labels: Total subperiosteal area; Medullary cavity area; Cortical area; *T*; *M*

fourth decade. *C* gains in thickness and area through
the fourth decade and then reverses as the medullary
cavity width (*M*) increases. Bone loss in adult life is
essentially a decrease in *C*, due to an age-associated
nonlinear increase in *M* but compensated in part by
a slow linear increase in *T* (Garn 1970).

Of primary interest for our hypothesis here is cortical bone, but *C* is the difference between *T* and *M*.
At times *M* outpaces *T* in expansion, and so *C* decreases. In later years, subperiosteal apposition increases *C* at the outer surface, while endosteal resorption simultaneously reduces *C* at the inner
surface. Thus, while the gain and loss of cortical
bone is of major concern, this necessarily concerns
the surface-specific changes, both subperiosteal, as
reflected by *T*, and endosteal, as measured by *M*.

Choice of Bone and Site

Radiogrammetric studies of changes in cortical
thickness, as derived by subtracting medullary cavity width from total subperiosteal diameter, are
most applicable when the tubular bone model holds.
The necessary measurements of *T* and *M* can be
made on radiographs of many tubular bones—the
femur, the tibia, the humerus, the radius, the meta-
carpals, and the metatarsals—but not all bones meet

the cylindrical model equally well. For living populations the second metacarpal is most commonly measured. Since this bone is not regularly recovered from archaeological samples, the femur, tibia, and humerus are employed from skeletal populations. From the King site, femurs and tibias were measured because of their superior preservation and the existence of comparable data from other southeastern archaeological sites. The femur is measured at the midpoint of the shaft, while the tibia is measured two-thirds the length of the bone from the distal end, following the general methodology employed by Hatch, Willey, and Hunt (1983).

Cortical Changes with Age and Malnutrition

Subperiosteal apposition, the growth of bone at the outer surface, during infancy and childhood resembles growth in length in that there is an early period of rapid increase and a later period of more moderate increase, continuing for a prolonged time until the onset of the adolescent growth spurt. This spurt is earlier in the female than in the male but larger in the male.

Subperiosteal apposition continues throughout life. The total width, T, is always larger in the late decades than in the third decade. The upward trend is small but consistent in both sexes. It is, moreover, relatively larger in the female than in the male (Garn 1970).

T is greater in the male than in the female at all ages from birth through the ninth decade in most living and skeletal populations (Garn 1970; Ericksen 1976). From the first through twelfth year of life, total subperiosteal diameter averages 4 percent greater in boys than in girls. For the remainder of the second decade, sexual dimorphism in T rises to 15 percent, about twice the adult sexual dimorphism in stature. From the beginning of the third decade on through the seventh decade, sexual dimorphism in the value T approximates 19 percent, a larger value than the sex difference in stature or bone lengths. At most ages the value of T is more variable in males than in females (Garn 1970).

Predictably, the value of T is less in cases of simple malnutrition. In protein-calorie malnutrition (PCM), the onset of the adolescent growth spurt is delayed, and adult values of the total subperiosteal diameter are reduced (Garn 1966). If we take total subperiosteal diameters for children and adults in the six Central American countries participating in the Central American Nutrition Survey, it is clear that T may be as much as 15 percent narrower in adults where malnutrition is common. The growth of T depends more upon caloric sufficiency than upon the availability of protein. Despite actual loss of bone at the endosteal surface and the reduction of as much as 40 percent of preformed bone (Garn et al. 1964; Garn 1966), growth at the subperiosteal surface in severe PCM is not necessarily diminished below that found in simple caloric deficiencies (Garn 1970).

The behavior of the subperiosteal surface at midshaft is relatively simple and primarily involves apposition rather than resorption though at a succession of different rates—perinatal, juvenile, adolescent, and adult. The behavior of the endosteal surface at midshaft is more complex. As measured by M, there is endosteal surface resorption until reversal occurs during the adolescent growth spurt, and then endosteal surface apposition follows until it is again reversed by the adult phase of endosteal bone loss, which persists from the end of the fourth decade to the end of life. M measures the labile surface that can be borrowed against and replaced (Garn 1970).

At all ages, M is larger in boys than in girls, and the rate of endosteal surface resorption is approximately 6 percent greater in the male through the end of the first decade. The linear rate of endosteal resorption shows a slightly larger sexual dimorphism than the corresponding linear rate of subperiosteal apposition.

As with T, changes in M are rapid during the first half year, followed by a slower juvenile rate of continuing endosteal resorption. In boys the juvenile resorptive phase continues well after the middle of the second decade. In girls the juvenile period lasts a shorter period of time (Garn 1970).

Following the adolescent growth spurt, the juvenile phase of increase ends and then reverses because of endosteal apposition. In the male adolescent, endosteal apposition is relatively small, but in the female it is rather large. Endosteal apposition from age fourteen to sixteen reduces medullary cavity width in the female to a narrower diameter than it was at the end of the fourteenth year. M reduces at least through age thirty in both sexes. This reduction is slight in males and greater in females. By age forty endosteal surface apposition is replaced by endosteal surface resorption, which continues to the end of life.

In cases of malnutrition, endosteal surface resorption may be excessive during childhood, adulthood, or both. In protein-calorie malnutrition, endosteal resorption is particularly excessive. Diagnosed cases of kwashiorkor—severe protein-calorie malnutrition—have greatly enlarged medullary cavities without much reduction in outer bone size (Garn 1966, 1970).

T measures changes at the outer bone surface, M

measures changes at the inner bone surface, and C $(T - M)$ reflects changes in net cortical thickness. Except for a very brief and transient period, C increases from earliest infancy through the fourth decade. C is ordinarily larger in the male, age for age, than in the female. C decreases, despite the continuing increase in T, after the fifth decade for all tubular bones. Cortical thickness is increased in pregnancy; it is decreased in protein-calorie malnutrition (Garn 1970).

Since T is only moderately restricted in PCM or not restricted at all, and the medullary cavity width is greatly increased because of a phenomenal rate of endosteal resorption, cortical thickness is in turn grossly reduced in both sexes (Garn 1970). Children with PCM are systematically below the appropriate norms for cortical thickness. Malnourished five-year-old children may have no more cortex than is normal for a one-year-old. Reduction in cortical thickness reflects actual bone loss rather than failure to form bone (Garn 1970).

Finally, cortical thickness is affected not only by nutritional status. C has genetic components that are expressed both between populations and within families (Smith et al. 1973). Mechanical loading tends to produce thicker cortexes (Ruff and Jones 1981). And many diseases affect cortical thickness, including some chromosomal abnormalities, congenital hemolytic anemia, osteogenesis imperfecta, rickets, and osteopetrosis (Garn 1972). For that reason grossly pathological bones were excluded from the present study.

Results and Discussion

On the basis of a preliminary survey of the King site population, it was hypothesized that a relative reduction in bone mass would be observed in several high-risk categories. Initial measurements of a small number of adults at the King site demonstrate a reduced tibial T and C as compared with adults recovered from the Alameda 329 skeletal collection housed in the Stanford University Museum. The Alameda 329 site is a San Francisco Bay shell mound dated to between A.D. 500 and 1000.

As might be expected, T is similar at both sites, while C is more seriously diminished at the King site. Differences between the two sites are more pronounced in males; the cortical and subperiosteal values are more variable in males. Sexual dimorphism is suppressed in the presence of malnutrition, acting to reduce diameters in males while affecting females less severely. These data are summarized in table 6.1.

From the expressions T, M, and C, the total subperiosteal area (TA), medullary cavity area (MA), and cortical area (CA) are computed. With total area (TA) and cortical area (CA) calculated, it is then simple to

Table 6.1   Total subperiosteal diameter and cortical diameter of tibias at the King and Alameda sites (millimeters)

	King	Alameda
Males[a]		
T	22.1	25.8
C	7.7	14.5
Females[b]		
T	19.5	21.6
C	7.7	10.4

Note: T = total subperiosteal diameter. C = cortical diameter.
[a]N = 18. [b]N = 10.

compute the percentage of cortical area (%CA). These formulas appear below.

$$TA = 0.785(T^2)$$
$$MA = 0.785(M^2)$$
$$CA = 0.785(T^2 - M^2)$$
$$\%CA = 100\left(\frac{T^2 - M^2}{T^2}\right)$$

As an area, TA has the advantage over T in that an absolutely small amount of subperiosteal apposition during childhood can make a sizable contribution to the total subperiosteal area. "Percentage of cortical area" simply describes the proportion of the total subperiosteal envelope that is composed of cortical bone. Cortical area is approximately 56 percent at age one. Thereafter %CA rises, reaching 80 percent by age twelve in both sexes (Garn 1970). During the adolescent growth spurt %CA rises further, exceeding 85 percent by age twenty but reaching a higher value in females than in males. After the fifth decade %CA decreases—at first slowly, then more rapidly. It decreases faster in females (Garn 1970).

In skeletons at the King site, TA, CA, and %CA are all low compared with the figures for Alameda males. The King site females have lower area values than Alameda females, but they are less reduced than for King site males. Apparently the King site inhabitants experienced some degree of suboptimal nutrient intake, although it is not at all clear to what extent. These data are summarized in table 6.2.

Subsequent comparisons of cortical bone thickness were made between the King sample and two native American skeletal series from the Georgia coast: a preagricultural group dating from 2200 B.C. to A.D. 1150 and an agricultural group dating from A.D. 1150 to 1550 (Larsen 1982; Ruff, Larsen, and

Table 6.2   Bone areas of tibias at the King and Alameda sites (square millimeters)

	King	Alameda
Males[a]		
TA	383	478
CA	219	365
%CA	57.2	76.1
Females[b]		
TA	319	365
CA	190	250
%CA	60.3	68.2

Note: TA = total subperiosteal area. CA = cortical area. %CA = percentage of cortical area.
[a]N = 18. [b]N = 10.

Table 6.3   Bone areas of femurs for King, coastal Georgia preagriculturalists, and coastal Georgia agriculturalists (square millimeters)

	TA	CA	MA
Males			
King[a]	603	494	109
Preagriculturalists[b]	568	420	148
Agriculturalists[c]	501	396	105
Females			
King[d]	502	404	110
Preagriculturalists[e]	488	326	162
Agriculturalists[f]	365	264	100

Note: TA = total subperiosteal area. CA = cortical area. MA = medullary cavity area.
[a]N = 17. [b]N = 8. [c]N = 11. [d]N = 16. [e]N = 12. [f]N = 9.

Hayes 1984; Blakely and Brown 1985). When compared with the samples from the Georgia coast, King site males and females exhibit larger cortical areas than both the preagricultural and the agricultural groups (table 6.3). In comparison with the preagriculturalists, King site individuals show the same total subperiosteal diameter, but the medullary cavity is smaller. In comparison with the agriculturalists, King site individuals have a greater total subperiosteal diameter, but the medullary cavity is the same (figure 6.3).

The transition from foraging to food production in many parts of the world was accompanied by a reduction in physical stress (Jurmain 1977; Larsen 1981; Cohen and Armelagos 1984). Since subperiosteal diameter reflects primarily mechanical loading, this is evident in the reduction of total subperiosteal diameter from the coastal preagriculturalists to the coastal agriculturalists (figure 6.3). Mechanical loading at King must have been similar to that of the coastal foragers, given the concordant figures for total subperiosteal diameter. It follows that activity levels were comparable. Because medullary area reflects primarily dietary protein sufficiency and general health, the data indicate that the diet at King was more adequate than that of either the coastal foragers or the food producers, although the similar values for medullary area suggest that protein sufficiency at King was closer to that of the agriculturalists. It may be inferred that the diet at King

Figure 6.3
Cortical bone thickness between coastal Georgia preagricultural ($N = 20$), King ($N = 33$), and coastal Georgia agricultural ($N = 20$) samples (not to scale)

Preagriculturalists   King   Agriculturalists

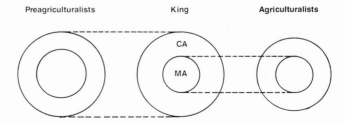

fell in between those for the coastal preagricultural and agricultural populations, supporting Kestle's conclusion that King's residents practiced a mixed subsistence economy.

Continuing investigations at King will explore the changes in cortical bone thickness from childhood through adolescence (Brown 1984) and will compare the data with those for additional southeastern skeletal populations.

Antoinette B. Brown

86

7

Stress and the
Battle Casualties

Bettina Detweiler-
Blakely

Lesions left by disease or trauma in the form of periostitis are often found on the skeletal remains of prehistoric American Indians (Wells 1964; Steinbock 1976; Ortner and Putschar 1981). Periosteal reactions were similarly diagnosed on the protohistoric King site remains, and comparisons were made with the Etowah skeletons in order to determine the relative extent of physiological stress occasioned by penetrating wounds, nutrition, indigenous infections, and the possible presence of European diseases.

Periostitis has been observed on Cretaceous dinosaur fossils as old as 100 million years; the periostitic response of bone is an ancient one (Wells 1964:77). A thin sheath of periosteum tissue covers all of the living bone except the cartilaginous ends and serves to feed nutrients into the compact bone, or cortex. The periosteum is sensitive to infection and trauma and responds by depositing layers of sclerotic bone (Brothwell 1965; Crouch 1965; Morse 1969; Steinbock 1976; Ubelaker 1978; Ortner and

Figure 7.1
Tibia of King site
Burial 74, a female in
her fifties, exhibiting
periosteal reaction at
the locus of a healed
wound

Putschar 1981). Consequently, all that can be observed on skeletal material is the bone response that has left behind a thickened area (figure 7.1). Since a wide range of factors can induce a periostitic response, it is best used as a qualitative tool to indicate general stress in a population. More often than not, periosteal reactions accompany pathologies affecting the inside of the bone as well; these normally include a pus-producing infection brought on primarily by staphylococci and streptococci microorganisms introduced into the blood through skin lacerations or by severe trauma (Brothwell 1965; Steinbock 1976).

A number of references document clinically diagnosed periostitis on specimens of recent origin and from archaeological sites (Cohen and Armelagos 1984). Steinbock (1976:60–61) and Ortner and Putschar (1981:129–132) describe the cellular process leading to periostitis and explain how causes such as infectious diseases and trauma may be single factors or may combine into multiple factors. Larsen (1982) and St. Hoyme and Bass (1962) have identified periostitis from sites once occupied by prehistoric native Americans and have analyzed its occurrence within the context of their subsistence patterns. Larsen's work on the Georgia coast compared disparate incidences of periosteal reactions between pre-agricultural and agricultural groups, for which he offers a number of possible explanations for the increase in incidence of periostitis among the agri-culturalists. The preagriculturalists were represented by older individuals and should therefore have increased opportunity for developing periostitis, but in fact they evidenced less periostitis than the agricultural sample. Adopting a new subsistence pattern from gathering and hunting to agriculture would increase the likelihood of introducing and maintaining diseases, but the effects on bones should be generalized rather than localized, as is normally the case in instances of trauma. Cases of periostitis in the sample of agriculturalists were usually too generalized to suggest that trauma accounted for their occurrence. According to Larsen, a more likely explanation for the greater incidence of periostitis among the agriculturalists is the shift in subsistence from foraging to food production. Apparently the change in subsistence from gathering and hunting to agriculture increased the prevalence of infections that produce suppurating wounds that would spread quickly and heal slowly under the more crowded and unsanitary conditions of the agriculturalists (see also Lallo and Blank 1977; Lallo, Armelagos, and Rose 1978; Cohen and Armelagos 1984).

In this context it is instructive to note the findings of St. Hoyme and Bass (1962), based on human skeletal remains from the Tollifero and Clarksville sites in the John H. Kerr Reservoir Basin in Virginia. The sites are geographically and ecologically similar and have occupations dating between 1000 B.C. and A.D. 500 for the Tollifero site and between A.D. 800 and 1630 for the Clarksville site. The earlier Tollifero site appears to represent a gathering and hunting society, as evidenced by worn teeth with relatively little decay. The teeth in the Clarksville remains, on the other hand, were generally very decayed. According to St. Hoyme and Bass (1962), a comparison of the skeletal remains from these two sites suggests that "the change from a hunting and gathering economy to an agricultural economy was at best a mixed blessing" (p. 394). There was a slight increase in stature and age in the Clarksville remains, but they had many more periostitic lesions, and their demineralized, curved tibias may be attributable to chronic nutritional deficiencies that lowered the people's resistance to disease and injury.

This chapter explores the causes of periosteal reactions at the King site and supports the conclusions reached by Larsen and St. Hoyme and Bass. In addition, cases of localized periostitis are correlated with healed wounds inflicted in battle with the Spaniards.

Materials and Methods

The skeletal sample examined consisted of 189 individuals. Of these, forty-nine were adult males, seventy-one were adult females, and sixty-nine were adults of indeterminate sex and unsexed juveniles. Following a procedure adopted by Blakely (1980) in analyzing the skeletons from Etowah, at least one-third of the bone from a skeleton had to be present before the individual could enter into the analysis.

Anything less was regarded as inadequate for evaluation to determine the presence or absence of periosteal reactions. This criterion reduced the sample to sixty-three individuals, including twenty-five males, twenty-six females, and twelve individuals of indeterminate sex. Analysis of remains at the King site entailed comparisons of the frequencies of periosteal reactions between several groups: individuals wounded and killed in battle, males and females, young and mature individuals, public burials and private burials, and King site remains evidencing no battle wounds as compared with the total Etowah samples. Samples were compared by chi-square tests (corrected for continuity when cell values were small); the .05 level of confidence was used to reject the null hypothesis that there were no significant differences between samples.

Results

Of the sixty-three sufficiently preserved skeletons, twelve were found to have bone lesions characteristic of periostitis. That is, 19 percent of the remains at the King site manifested periostitis. When compared with Etowah's 14 percent (Blakely 1980), the difference is not statistically significant. What is statistically significant ($\chi^2 = 10.461$, $p < .01$) is the association between periostitis and individuals who showed evidence of healed wounds (figure 7.2). Of eleven individuals who survived severe injuries (their wounds exhibiting signs of healing), seven had cases of periostitis, but twenty-six individuals killed immediately (that is, with wounds exhibiting no signs of healing) included only three cases of periostitis. (The appendix to this volume lists all individuals diagnosed as periostitic along with those evidencing healed and unhealed wounds.) In other

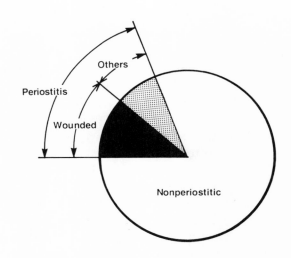

Figure 7.2
Nineteen percent of
the King sample
(N = 63) exhibited
periosteal reactions.
Of those, more than
half (11 percent) evi-
denced healed
wounds, with the re-
mainder (8 percent)
attributable to other
causes.

words, 64 percent of those with healed wounds had
periostitis, whereas only 11 percent of those with
unhealed wounds had periostitis. *The association
between periostitis and wounded survivors is highly significant statistically* (see table 7.1). The incidence of periostitis among the wounded survivors
can likely be linked to greater susceptibility to infectious diseases resulting from bone-penetrating injuries. When this segment of the burial population is
removed from the rest of the skeletal sample, the
frequency of periosteal reactions drops to 8 percent.
Among Etowahns, the incidence of periosteal reactions is 75 percent greater than at King (14 percent
versus 8 percent), suggesting that different forces, or
the same forces to different degrees, were operating
to produce periosteal reactions at the two sites.

Because periostitis is age-progressive, all samples
were tested by age categories to see if there was a
correlation between age and incidences of periostitis. There is in fact a significant difference ($\chi^2 =$
$4.929, p < .05$) in the incidence of periostitis for subadults under seventeen years and adults seventeen

years and over. No subadults evidenced periostitis. Tests between adults over thirty-six and under thirty-six disclosed no significant differences. The ratio of males to females with periosteal reactions was 3 : 1 (nine to three). The healed-wound sample included five males and two females with periosteal reactions. Comparisons of periostitis frequencies between the private and public sectors at King revealed no significant differences, whereas at Etowah, high-status burials included 11 percent with periostitis and low-status burials included 19 percent with periostitis.

Discussion

The incidences of periosteal reactions at the King site nicely fit Mathews's (1984b) interpretation of remains evidencing trauma. He concluded that many of King's inhabitants were involved in a battle with the Spaniards that left a variety of marks on their bones. Mathews found that some wounds inflicted by edged metal weapons were accompanied by bone remodeling, while other wounds inflicted by edged metal weapons were not accompanied by bone remodeling. Individuals with remodeling apparently survived their injuries at least long enough for the

Table 7.1   Association between periosteal reactions and wounded survivors

	Periostitic	Nonperiostitic	N
Wounded survivors	7	4	11
Others	5	47	52
Total	12	51	63

Note: $\chi^2 = 17.126$, $p < .001$; significant. The chi-square test was corrected for continuity.

bones to react, whereas those with no bone changes were probably killed immediately. The high incidence of periosteal reactions among those with healed wounds (64 percent) lends support to Mathews's diagnoses of wounded survivors and those fatally injured. Moreover, the most common sites of periostitic lesions were areas localized on the tibia—one of the two bones identified by Mathews as most frequently injured. Eight of the twelve cases of periostitis implicate the tibias, and of these, five have periosteal reactions on one tibia only. This finding would seem to rule out contagious diseases as the cause, since pathogens carried through the blood tend to affect bone in a more generalized and bilateral manner than infections introduced by trauma (Steinbock 1976:60).

What activities other than warfare could be responsible for trauma-induced periostitis? Wells (1964:99), Ortner and Putschar (1981:130), Zimmerman and Kelley (1982:99), and Živanović (1982:221) note that under *most* circumstances tibias are more often afflicted with periostitis than other bones because the close proximity of the bone to the surface of the skin makes it more susceptible to injury. Explanations for the causes of injury to the lower leg range from types of clothing worn to the types of physical activity involved in obtaining subsistence requirements. Wells (1964:79) even suggested the possibility that the Bodega Head people from southern India subjected their legs to injury by climbing on slippery rocks in search of clams. But the above explanations seem unsatisfactory for the remains at the King site because the incidence of periosteal reactions decreases significantly when it is not associated with healed wounds that are morphologically similar to the fatal injuries. In fact, when the healed-wound sample is removed from the total sample for the King site and is compared with Etowah, the difference in incidences of periostitis is highly statistically significant ($\chi^2 = 14.605$, $p < .001$). The three cases of periostitis from the unhealed sample (that is, people who were killed) were included in this comparison because they obviously experienced stress that took place prior to and disassociated from their deaths. The low incidence of periosteal reactions at the King site suggests either of two possibilities: (1) that the people experienced lower levels of stress than the Etowahns or (2), paradoxically, that they were exposed to higher levels of acute disorders than the Etowahns. Let us first consider the latter alternative.

Low levels of nonspecific stress indicators such as periostitis may actually reflect a high prevalence of acute systemic diseases because virulent disorders rarely leave bone lesions. This is either because they kill the victim before the skeleton has a chance to react or because the victim recovers too soon for bone involvement (Ortner 1979). Since these diseases are often fatal, a test for their presence in once-living populations is evidence of low levels of nonspecific stress combined with high levels of mortality in at-risk groups. The highest rates of morbidity and mortality typically occur in the very young, the aged, and young adults (Black 1980; Garruto 1981). The fifteen-to-twenty-five age group may be particularly susceptible, apparently because its T-immunity system intensifies symptomatic responses to the invading microorganism (Burnet and White 1972).

At the King site, low levels of periostitis are associated with *low mortality* in the highest at-risk groups. Although mortality peaks in the first, third, and fifth decades (see figure 2.2), the apexes in the twenties, forties, and fifties are largely artifacts of the battle; when these fatalities are excluded, the mortality profile is not unlike that of epidemic-free populations. Therefore, the low incidence of periostitis probably does not indicate high levels of acute disorders. The implication is also that European diseases did not catastrophically reduce King's numbers, an argument that Blakely and I have further developed elsewhere (Blakely and Detweiler-Blakely 1985).

The alternative hypothesis—that the low incidence of periostitis reflects low levels of physiologic stress—is accepted and discussed below. The sample size is too small to offer solid evidence for frequency differences between males and females with periostitis, especially if those wounded in battle are deleted from the sample. Mathews's (1984b) sample of remains afflicted by trauma contains thirty-seven individuals—twenty-six killed and eleven wounded. The wounded segment included seven males, five of whom had periostitis, and four females, two of whom had periostitis. The unwounded sample with periosteal reactions consisted of four males and one female. Larsen's study of skeletal lesions among preagriculturalists from archaeological sites along the Georgia coast indicates that neither males nor females were more susceptible to chronic infections manifested in bone, even though there appear to have been sex role differences (1982:252–253).

Among seventeen individuals under seventeen years of age in the sample, no cases of periostitis were found. The implication is that subadults experienced little stress from either inadequate nutrition or infectious diseases. Although Blakely (see chapter 2) discovered elevated mortality at the age of weaning, data derived from enamel hypoplasias support the inference that children at King enjoyed comparatively good health. Enamel hypoplasias, which have been associated with nutritional stress and systemic disorders (Clarke 1978; El-Najjar, DeSanti, and Ozebek 1978; Goodman, Armelagos, and Rose 1980), peak at age four among those surviving to adulthood at both King and Etowah. Among subadults, however, the incidence of enamel hypoplasias is two and one-half times greater at Etowah than at King, leading Blakely and me (1985) to conclude that King's children were spared many of the severe nutritional insults and debilitating infectious diseases that raised morbidity and mortality among Etowah's children.

We have already seen that the frequency and degree of periostitis varies according to the type of subsistence pattern practiced. Gatherer/hunters tend to have low incidences of periostitis, whereas populations incorporating both gathering/hunting and agriculture experience mild degrees of periostitis in high frequencies. Agricultural populations have either high rates of periostitis in mild forms (due to low-grade infections) or low rates of periostitis in extreme forms (due to severe infections). As previously noted, when a highly infectious disease produces death quickly, evidence seldom remains on the skeleton, indicating that the disease met little resistance. A more adaptable mechanism for both the host and the infection-producing microorganism is an immune response that permits the development of a chronic condition resulting in noticeable bone remodeling. The low incidence (and mild expression) of periosteal reactions at the King site most closely matches the model for foragers. Kestle and Brown (see chapters 5 and 6) note, however, that the odontological, trace element, and cortical bone data strongly suggest a mixed subsistence economy. Perhaps gathering and hunting were emphasized.

Cassidy (1984) and Norr (1984) have found 25 percent to be about the average figure for periostitic lesions from archaeological gathering/hunting societies in North America. King's 8 percent falls far short of this expected frequency. This I attribute to adequate nutrition provided by foraging supplemented by agriculture, low levels of indigenous infections, and the absence of European diseases.

Summary

At first glance, the overall incidence of periosteal reactions at the King site would seem to indicate that the residents lived in a more stress-filled environment than the Etowahns. However, that segment of the burial population which survived wounds sustained in battle with the Spaniards constitutes the majority of the cases of periostitis. When the battle victims are removed from the periostitis sample, the incidence drops to an unusually low frequency, indicating there was little episodic stress at King. Subadult remains exhibit no periostitis; of the few adults afflicted, males predominated. The low level of periostitis suggests that nutrition was generally adequate, chronic infections were uncommon, European diseases were absent, and trauma was infrequent beyond that occasioned by the Spanish encounter.

Bettina Detweiler-
Blakely

III

The Spanish Encounter

8

The Massacre: The Discovery of De Soto in Georgia

David S. Mathews

Examination of the skeletal remains at the King site in search of evidence for disease and trauma revealed a number of unhealed cuts, healed injuries, and animal bite marks. Observed injuries include nineteen cut marks, which are primarily clean cuts into the bone at angles of 45 degrees or less, five puncture injuries, and bite marks on twenty-one individuals. In attempting to interpret the nature of these injuries, I used information on wound distribution over the body, population mortality, disease prevalence and distribution, bite mark analysis, burial distribution and status, and comparisons with European battle injuries. I then compared these data and known Spanish activities in the area.

The distribution of unhealed and healed injuries shows that both types of lesions were predominantly in the legs (figure 8.1). Sixty-six percent of all fatal injuries and 74 percent of all healed injuries were located in the legs. The total number of injuries exceeds the number of casualties because some indi-

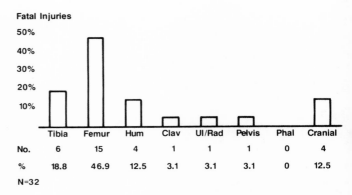

Fatal Injuries

	Tibia	Femur	Hum	Clav	Ul/Rad	Pelvis	Phal	Cranial
No.	6	15	4	1	1	1	0	4
%	18.8	46.9	12.5	3.1	3.1	3.1	0	12.5

N=32

Figure 8.1
Healed and unhealed
injuries, showing
distribution on the
skeleton

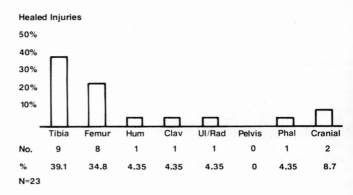

Healed Injuries

	Tibia	Femur	Hum	Clav	Ul/Rad	Pelvis	Phal	Cranial
No.	9	8	1	1	1	0	1	2
%	39.1	34.8	4.35	4.35	4.35	0	4.35	8.7

N=23

viduals sustained multiple wounds. The bone-by-bone distributions are quite similar but were too small for statistical comparisons. Both cut marks and healed injuries occur on the tibia, femur, humerus, ulna, radius, and cranium (figures 8.2 and 8.3). The similar distribution supports the proposition that both the cut marks and the healed injuries were products of the same activity, which I shall show was a battle between some of King's inhabitants and a Spanish expeditionary force.

The incidence and locations on the skeleton of healed wounds at King were markedly different from their incidence and locations at Etowah. Twenty-nine cases of healed traumatic injuries were found in the King site material, compared with eight in the Etowah village sample (Blakely 1980). Seventeen of the King site injuries were to the legs, as compared with one for Etowah. If we take into account differences in the population size, the rate of occurrence of healed injuries is three times greater at the King site than at Etowah. The proposition that the King site inhabitants were exceptionally clumsy and accident prone is not very tenable.

Preliminary analyses of the age breakdown of the burial population at the King site raised the possibility of an "unusual" mortality distribution (Tally 1974; Funkhouser 1978). Blakely and I found support for this assertion. Putative battle victims fell largely into two categories: females in their twenties and men and women in their forties and fifties. The mor-

Figure 8.2
Three fatal wounds inflicted by an edged metal weapon on the femur of Burial 55, an elderly female

tality rates were then examined to see the effects of removing those individuals classified as battle victims. Their removal caused the mortality curve to move sharply toward a more typical population curve for the area (Blakely and Mathews 1975), but it

Figure 8.3
Fatal wound inflicted by an edged metal weapon on the cranium of Burial 23, a male in his fifties

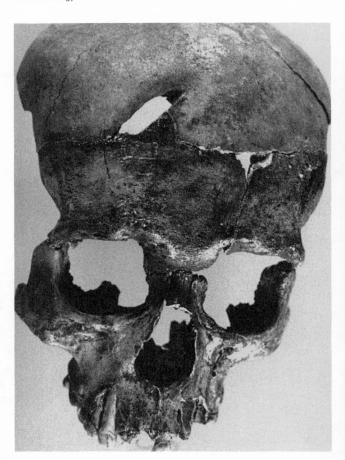

David S. Mathews

did not remove all of the nonstable aspects of the mortality curve (see chapter 2). While the battle victims had a definite effect on the resulting population mortality, the possibility exists that other disruptive factors could have been at work.

The diseased condition most extensively studied in the King site remains is periostitis (Detweiler-Blakely 1984). As Detweiler-Blakely noted, almost two-thirds of the periostitis cases were found among eleven individuals who had previously been classified as surviving wounded. This provided independent verification of the classification derived from the healed injuries themselves. The very high rate of periostitis would be explained if the healed injuries were healed cuts rather than healed fractures, as cuts would be more likely to expose the bone to the air and would thus stand a good chance of infection. Furthermore, not one of the injuries classified as healed cuts exhibits angular deformity or healing completely around the bone, as would be expected with at least a portion of a group of healed fractures.

Twenty-one individuals had small scratches or gnawings (usually a number were present) that have been identified as animal bite marks. They were made by rats, possums, and possibly by fish (figure 8.4). Eleven of these individuals are in the group of battle victims (figure 8.5). A chi-square test corrected for continuity indicated that the association between the battle casualties and the occurrence of bite marks is statistically significant beyond the .001 level of confidence (figure 8.6 and table 8.1). (The appendix to this volume lists all individuals wounded and killed in battle with the Spaniards, along with the incidences of animal bite marks and cases of periosteal reactions.)

The importance of the bite marks, besides adding evidence that the battle-group classification is cor-

Figure 8.4
Top: rat gnawings on a bone from Burial 149, a fatally wounded
female in her forties. Bottom: rat gnawings on a modern bone.

rect, is that it is consistent with our knowledge that
the bodies were left exposed and unattended for several days after they were killed in the only documented Spanish/Indian battle in the area. The profu-
sion and depth of some of the bites suggest that the
bodies were probably exposed for many days.

The spatial distribution of the burials of all killed
and wounded individuals and the poorly preserved
individuals with bite marks only was plotted on a
map of the site (Hally 1975c). The most striking feature of this plotting is that the distributions of the
three categories are the same. Most significantly, individuals with bite marks only are never found away
from the areas where the fatally wounded were in-

terred. Therefore, the individuals with bite marks only were probably killed in battle too.

Alternative explanations for the animal bite marks—that they are the result of burrowing animals after interment or represent scavenger activity on corpses placed in charnel houses—are not supported by the data. Because of the statistical correlation between bite marks and fatal injuries, the former explanation would force one to conclude that animals burrowed selectively into the graves of massacre victims. For the same reason, the latter explanation would presuppose that victims of the battle made up the bulk of those consigned to charnel houses. Virtually all of the remains exhibiting bite marks and fatal wounds were found in low-ranking

Figure 8.5
Fatal wounds on either side of possum gnawings on the femur of Burial 1, a female in her forties

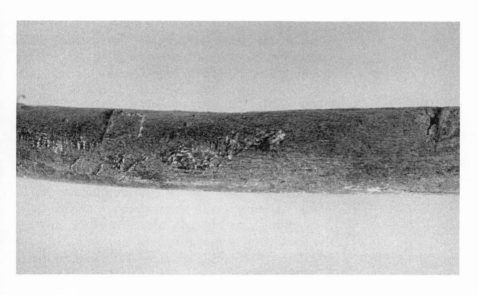

Figure 8.6
Analysis of the King
sample (*N* = 189),
showing percentages
wounded, with fatal
wounds, and with
animal bite marks

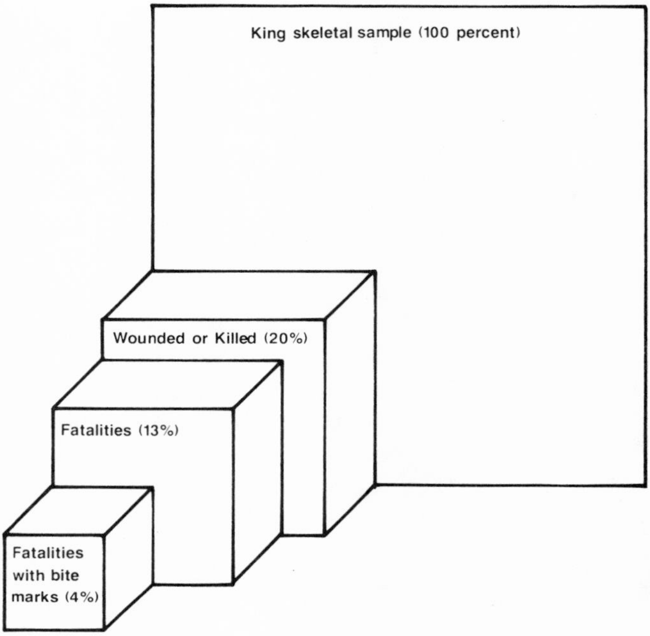

King skeletal sample (100 percent)

Wounded or Killed (20%)

Fatalities (13%)

Fatalities
with bite
marks (4%)

burials. Elsewhere in the Southeast, such postmortem treatment was reserved for high-ranking individuals (Hudson 1976). Thus the facts at King are at odds with the notion that the bite marks are evidence of either burrowing into burials or scavenger activity in charnel houses.

Five groups of burials containing battle casualties appear on the King site plotting, all associated with clusters of houses. They are separated by structures that contain no battle casualties. These clusters were likely lineage-based groupings of structures, suggesting that the victims were confined to particular kin groups. It is important to note in this regard that, among these burials, all of which occurred at the same time, some groupings show burial outside dwellings, while other groupings show burial inside dwellings (Hally, Garrow, and Trotti 1975). In other words, mortuary patterns are not consistent over the site (Seckinger 1975). This characteristic appears to be lineage related rather than an indication of temporal change in burial practices.

With the exception of five burials located in the plaza and ceremonial structure, all graves containing battle victims occur in low-status areas. That most of the residents involved in the battle were of low status will become significant later in this chapter.

On the assumption that wounds appearing on the King site remains and on the remains of a European battle sample should be similar, since both were purportedly inflicted by European soldiery, I compared injuries from the King site with injuries from the late medieval Battle of Wisby in Denmark. The mass graves of Wisby held fifteen hundred of the fallen, and the injuries have been previously analyzed in connection with research into the battle practices of the period (Thordeman 1939).

At the Danish site, as well as at the Georgia site, the two main types of injuries are cuts and punctures. Seventy-eight percent of the wounds from both Wisby and King are cut marks. Blows to the legs constitute the majority of injuries in both cases.

Table 8.1   Association between bite marks and battle casualties

	Bite marks absent	Bite marks present	N
Fatal injuries	17	9	26
Healed injuries	9	2	11
Others	142	10	152
Total	168	21	189

Note: $\chi^2 = 15.804$ (2 df), $p < .001$; significant. The chi-square test was corrected for continuity.

Two important differences are revealed by the depth and distribution of the cuts. The cuts at the King site are less severe, and femur cuts predominate; at Wisby, the cuts are deeper, and tibia cuts predominate.

Tibia cuts have been analyzed for both Wisby and King, so that a more detailed comparison is possible. Both sets of tibias showed the largest number of cuts on the front and the fewest on the rear of the bone. They were also primarily cuts from above, although cuts from below were more common at the King site than at Wisby. The major difference between the two sets of cuts is their location on the bone. If we divide the tibia into upper and lower halves, Wisby's injuries occur more often distally, while at the King site cuts occur more often proximally.

To summarize, in comparing wounds at the two sites to see whether the pattern of injuries at King matches the pattern observed from a European battle, one sees several striking similarities: types of wounds, frequency of wound types, and distribution over the body. There are also two major differences.

The first difference is the location of injuries on the femur and upper tibia at King and on the lower tibia at Wisby. This can be explained by a difference in equipment. At Wisby, many, if not most, of the fallen carried heavy shields which would have protected the upper tibia and femur. The second difference is the less severe nature of injuries from the King site, which can again be explained by the equipment. The majority of the combatants at Wisby were armored, and undoubtedly many of the heavier weapons designed to cut and pierce armor were in use. The presence of such weapons—two-handed axes, two-handed swords, and maces—has not been documented in the southeastern United States. In any event they would not have been needed to fight unshielded Indians.

This comparison, then, reveals only those differences that one would expect from the different arms used in the two battles. Therefore, the King site wounds could well have resulted from the actions of a European trained army. The age and sex composition of the battle victims corroborates this conclusion and offers further evidence that other Indians, using weapons traded from—or taken from—the Spaniards, could not have been responsible for the violence.

As already mentioned, battle casualties from the King site fall into two age categories, the twenties and the forties and fifties (figure 2.3). All but one individual in the younger group are females. Those in their forties and fifties are divided almost equally between males and females. The distribution by age and sex is as notable for its exclusions as for its inclusions. No injuries were sustained by children recovered at the site. And no one identified by Garrett (1984) as belonging to the warrior class had healed or unhealed wounds. Because the sample of battle casualties is demographically and socially unrepresentative of the burial population as a whole, some groups of people were selectively forced into or drawn into participation in the conflict. The absence of children and warriors strongly suggests that the battle did not take place in the immediate vicinity of the site. Moreover, since southeastern Indians seldom killed females—they usually captured women and killed warriors (Hudson 1976)—the inclusion of so many females in the wounded and killed sample indicates that the perpetrators were not Indian but Spanish.

Research into the three major expeditions that are known to have visited the area brought to light one battle that appears to match the information gleaned from the King site remains. That is the Battle of Mabila, which took place in Alabama between Hernando de Soto and the Indians of Coosa and Tascaluza on October 18, 1540 (Lowery 1901, 1959; Priestly 1928, 1936; Quinn 1977). According to De Soto's chroniclers, no military engagements involving loss of life occurred within the province of Coosa, but many slaves were taken in Coosa, and it was not De Soto's habit to release them (U.S. De Soto Commission 1939).

On Friday, August 20, 1540, De Soto left the town of Coosa. From there he went to Itaba, believed by Hudson et al. (Chiefdom, 1985, 1987) to be the Etowah site. From Etowah he marched to Ulibahali. Here he was met by armed Indians who had gathered to free their chief. The chief of Coosa defused the situation and gave to De Soto more bearers (age and sex unspecified) and twenty or thirty women as concubines for De Soto's men (DePratter, Hudson, and Smith 1985).

Ulibahali is described as being located on a river, with a stream nearby. It was surrounded by a ten- or twelve-foot palisade of large timbers with crossbars and embrasures. It was coated inside and out with clay, but loopholes had been left for archery. An estimated twenty-five to thirty miles farther downriver, De Soto again took bearers and female slaves (DePratter, Hudson, and Smith 1985). Five days farther south De Soto was in the next province and freed the chief of Coosa. He stayed there twenty days. After passing through three more villages, De Soto arrived at Athahachi, where Tascaluza, a high chief, was taken captive. Two days out from Athahachi, at Piache, one of De Soto's men disappeared. Supposedly to make reparations, Tascaluza sent a runner to have provisions prepared for De Soto at the next town, but the runner was really sent to call nearby villages to arms (Bourne 1904).

De Soto's advance guard reached Mabila on Monday, October 18, 1540. Fifteen cavalry and thirty infantry accompanied De Soto into the village. On the pretext of speaking to some of his subordinate chiefs, Tascaluza entered a house that was filled with armed warriors and refused to come out. Angered, one of De Soto's men pulled the marten skin cloak off of one of the chiefs in the plaza and cut him down the back with his sword. The warriors of Mabila fell on De Soto. De Soto was wounded and five of his men were killed trying to escape from the village (Bourne 1904).

The Indians, while chasing De Soto through the palisade, freed De Soto's slaves, who had been stationed outside the palisade. The slaves were then armed and turned to fight the Spanish. Most of De Soto's supplies were being carried by the slaves, including about half of the Spanish weapons, which were subsequently lost to the expedition in the course of the battle (Bourne 1904).

De Soto's cavalry made a small counterattack, lancing a few Indians and driving them back into the village. De Soto's main body proceeded to surround the village. Tascaluza escaped as this maneuver was under way. The fighting was apparently lengthy. Several times De Soto entered the town and was driven out. In the end the Spaniards were victorious and the town was burned. The Spaniards listed the death toll at 18 Spanish dead, 150 Spanish wounded, and 2,500 Indians dead (Bourne 1904). One account states that all of De Soto's slaves were killed in the battle. De Soto camped near Mabila for another month to repair arms and equipment and to allow wounds to heal before heading west.

One of the objectives of the present analysis was to match skeletal and historical data. As to the existence of a sample of battle casualties, the high frequency of healed and unhealed wounds—similar in both morphology and location on the skeleton—offers evidence of killed and injured battle victims. Detweiler-Blakely's analysis of periostitis helped to show that many healed wounds had resulted from open cuts rather than fractures. The comparison with European battle casualties demonstrated that the wounds probably reflected battle tactics of a European army. And the mortality pattern of the battle-victims sample is socially and demographically unrepresentative of the King site population.

De Soto took unspecified bearers and young women for sexual pleasures. The age/sex breakdown of the battle victims shows females in their early twenties and men and women in their forties and fifties. This breakdown is consistent with De Soto's known slave taking. Also, the individuals appear to have been chosen from only certain low-status lineages. They were definitely not a random sampling of the village population. In fact, they closely match the description of slaves taken by De Soto at Ulibahali, which has been placed within twenty miles of the King site (Garrow 1975; Hudson et al., *Chiefdom*, 1985, 1987).

We know that slaves were taken in Coosa and died at Mabila (Bourne 1904). The fatalities from King appear to represent the segments of the population taken by De Soto as slaves. The animal bite marks indicate that the bodies were exposed sometime before burial. De Soto not only burned the town of Mabila, killing all who did not escape, but camped nearby for some time with his army. It is therefore unlikely that the Indians could have recovered the bodies quickly and highly improbable that De Soto would have bothered with them.

European tools and weapons of the period have been recovered from the King site (Smith 1975). The sword found at King is of early enough manufacture to have been carried on the De Soto expedition

(Helmut Nickel, Metropolitan Museum of Art, to Keith Little 1982). And Mabila is the only battle of the expedition at which any arms are recorded as having been lost.

The final question is: under what name did De Soto know the King site? The answer here is the most tentative. There are really two possibilities. One is that the current placement of Ulibahali underestimates De Soto's rate of travel and that the King site is itself Ulibahali, where many slaves are said to have been taken. The other possibility is that the King site is an unnamed town that was under the jurisdiction of Ulibahali to the south. This possibility to be valid would mean that many men and women from this village were at Ulibahali when De Soto arrived.

On the basis of the known killed and wounded individuals, individuals bearing bite marks, and multiple graves—all of which contained battle victims—the best estimate of those killed and wounded from the King site is sixty.[1] Given the large number of interred casualties, the King site must have been a village from which slaves were taken directly. Also, the written description of Ulibahali fits the King site (Hally 1975a, 1975b). Moreover, because no massive, unrecorded battle is presupposed, it is the most parsimonious answer.

I state this conclusion hesitantly for two reasons. First, the other possible sites for Ulibahali have not been sufficiently explored to see whether they match the known information as well as the King site. Second, in the course of our investigation of the King site, simpler explanations made as work progressed generally turned out to be wrong.

Although researchers may continue to argue about the details of what De Soto did, the De Soto expedition through Georgia has at least been discovered. Part of its route has been mapped, and some of its activities have been exposed. We have found the first known Indian victims, a very few of the many casualties left by De Soto and his army.

Notes

1. *Editor's note:* Mathews's figure is a maximum one, since it includes inferred as well as observed casualties. A low estimate is about forty. Roughly half of the King site burial population was archaeologically recovered. There is no reason to suspect that battle victims were confined to the excavated portion of the site, so the number of casualties exceeds either estimate. Because King was occupied for approximately two generations, one can assume that in numbers one generation is represented by the analyzed remains. It stands to reason that the generation that witnessed the battle lost between one-third and one-half of its members to De Soto's army.

David S. Mathews
116

9

The Victims of the King Site Massacre: A Historical Detectives' Report

*Charles Hudson,
Chester DePratter,
and Marvin Smith*

When Patrick Garrow conducted preliminary excavations at the King site, he saw what he interpreted as evidence that some of the inhabitants of the site had died violently. Subsequent excavation turned up additional evidence of violent death (Hally 1975a; Seckinger 1975). However, not until the detailed study of the skeletal remains from the King site by Robert L. Blakely and David S. Mathews (see chapter 8) were the nature and frequency of the injuries fully appreciated. Far more individuals at the King site suffered wounds and death from violence than was at first apparent, and the nature and frequencies of the wounds they suffered, plus the fact that in some cases their bodies were exposed for a time before they were buried, suggest that they were the victims of a European military action. The question, as Sherlock Holmes might have phrased it,

We are grateful to David Hally for reading and criticizing this paper.

is: "Who, my dear Watson, perpetrated this massacre?"

When the King site was excavated, it showed itself to be a single-component site which was occupied for a relatively short period of time—twenty-five to fifty years at most. On the basis of European artifacts which were recovered when the site was excavated, this period of occupation was determined to have been in the middle of the sixteenth century. Recently, Marvin Smith has developed a more refined classification of early European trade goods. If we use his classification, the King site can be dated from about 1540 to about 1565 (Smith 1987).

Smith has also adduced evidence that many sites in the general area of the King site were abandoned in the latter half of the sixteenth century, after Old World diseases had begun taking their toll. Although the timing of the earliest epidemics is still uncertain, the King site could have been abandoned after an epidemic of an unknown disease which appears to have occurred between 1564 and 1570 (Smith 1987). It can be inferred that the King site was occupied from about 1535 until about 1570.

Several minor expeditions and three major expeditions of European explorers penetrated into the interior of the Southeast between 1539 and 1600. The French under René de Laudonnière sent exploratory parties to the "Apalatchy Mountains" in the 1560s. These expeditions consisted of only five or six soldiers each, and they depended on friendly relations with the Indians for freedom of movement (Le Moyne 1965:48). It is doubtful that any of these reached the piedmont, much less the mountains. In 1597, Governor Méndez de Canzo of the Province of Florida sent a party consisting of two priests and a soldier to Tama in interior Georgia, but they encountered no hostility (Quinn 1979:93–94, 96–98).

This expedition probably penetrated only to Piedmont Georgia. The Spaniards also sent several small expeditions into the interior between 1600 and 1630 (Bolton and Ross 1925:18), but if our dating of the King site is accurate, they were too late to have been responsible for the King site massacre.

Our list of suspects is thus reduced to three: the expeditions led by Hernando de Soto in 1539–1543, Tristán de Luna in 1559–1561, and Juan Pardo in 1566–1568. Let us proceed by eliminating suspects.

Juan Pardo led an expedition of just over one hundred infantry into the interior of the Carolinas in late 1566 (DePratter, Hudson, and Smith 1983). Departing from Santa Elena, near present-day Beaufort, South Carolina, they traveled as far as Joara (De Soto's Xuala), which we have located on the upper Catawba River in the vicinity of Marion, North Carolina. They had been ordered to go all the way to the Spanish silver mines in Zacatecas, Mexico, but because it had already snowed before they reached Joara, they could not cross the mountains. Pardo built a small fort at Joara, and he left Sergeant Hernando Moyano de Morales with thirty men to occupy and defend it. Moyano remained there until April of 1567, when an Indian chief, probably a Chisca, threatened him. Moyano then crossed the mountains with twenty of his men and destroyed the Indian chief's town. He proceeded southward to Chiaha (or Olameco), a town which was located on Zimmerman's Island, near Dandridge, Tennessee. From here Moyano explored farther, but he probably did not go very far from Chiaha because the Indians became hostile, and he and his men were surrounded.

In the fall of 1567, Pardo led another force of infantry into the interior, again reached Joara, and immediately crossed the mountains to relieve Moyano at

Chiaha (figure 9.1). When Pardo and his men reached Chiaha, they rested briefly and then continued in a southwestward direction, heading, they thought, toward Zacatecas. But they went no farther than two towns on the upper Little Tennessee River, where a large force of Indians waited to oppose their passage. Thinking it prudent to avoid an armed encounter, Pardo turned around and returned to Chiaha. Here he built another small fort, left a small contingent of soldiers to man it, and recrossed the mountains with the remainder of his army (Hudson 1987).

Since the main body of Pardo's army went no farther south than the Little Tennessee River, his men could not have perpetrated the massacre at the King site. Pardo's notary, Juan de la Bandera, wrote a brief report on the expedition in which he summarizes some information that an informant gave him on Indian towns to the south of the Little Tennessee River, extending all the way to Tascaluza in central Alabama (Folmsbee and Lewis 1965:120–121). But Bandera does not identify his informant, nor does he describe the circumstances under which his informant obtained this information. This information may have been obtained from an excursion by one or more men who were with Moyano at Chiaha before Pardo arrived, though this is doubtful in light of the fact that Moyano was surrounded and threatened by the Indians of Chiaha. But even if Moyano's men had succeeded in traveling southward to the King site, they would have been too few to have carried out the massacre.

Our next suspect is the Tristán de Luna expedition (figure 9.1). Luna attempted to establish a colony at Pensacola in 1559, but his colony was badly planned and ill-fated. When his people began to starve, Luna moved his colony inland to an Indian town on the Alabama River. From here he sent out a party of

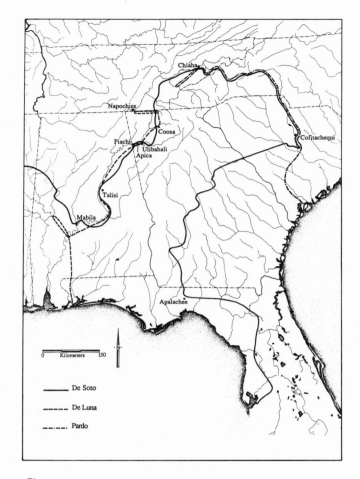

Figure 9.1
Portions of the routes taken by three Spanish explorers: Hernando de Soto in 1540, Tristán de Luna in 1560, and Juan Pardo in 1567 (second expedition)

about forty cavalry and one hundred infantry to go northward to find the province of Coosa, which had been visited previously by the De Soto expedition (Priestly 1928). It was known to be a rich province with plenty of food. The King site was one of the member towns of this province of Coosa, or, more properly, the chiefdom of Coosa (figure 9.2).

This party of cavalry and infantry set out on April 15, 1560, to find the main town of the chiefdom of Coosa. Several men who had been members of the De Soto expedition were among Luna's army, and they were in the party he sent to Coosa. Debilitated by hardship and starvation, and following the trails with difficulty, they began inching their way northward, revisiting some of the towns De Soto had visited. Just before they reached Ulibahali, which was in or near Rome, Georgia, they came to a village named Apica. This was on or about July 6. We believe this town to have been at the Johnstone Farm site, which is about halfway between Rome and the King site. Here they obtained some food from the Indians, and they remained at this place for several days. Some of these soldiers may have visited the King site, which is about eleven miles from the Johnstone Farm site. Or if they did not actually visit the site, they may have traded with or otherwise dealt with Indians who lived at the King site. Some of the European artifacts excavated at the King site may well have been obtained from Luna's men.

Luna's men continued on to Ulibahali and then to the main town of the chiefdom of Coosa, which was at the Little Egypt site at Carters, Georgia (Hudson et al., *Chiefdom*, 1985). While they were at the main town of Coosa, the chief of Coosa persuaded Luna's men to send fifty of their number along with his own warriors on a raid against the Napochies, a tributary group who were refusing to pay tribute to

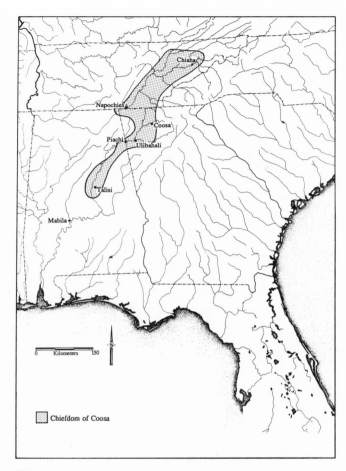

Figure 9.2
Map of the paramount chiefdom of Coosa in the sixteenth century

Coosa. The party of Indians and Spaniards traveled for two long days before reaching the first town of Napochies. Two leagues beyond this first town they came to a second Napochie town on a very large river which was said to have been "two arquebus [matchlock] shots wide." It could only have been the Tennessee River, and the towns were probably in the vicinity of present-day Chattanooga. The Napochies had somehow learned that the Coosas were coming, and they fled their villages. The Coosas and their Spanish allies inflicted only light casualties on the Napochies (Hudson n.d.).

Beyond this encounter, there is no evidence that Luna's men inflicted any casualties on the Indians of Coosa. Moreover, because Luna's men were conciliatory toward the Indians, giving them gifts and barter in exchange for food, there is reason to think that Luna's men took pains to avoid injuring the Indians. For example, while they were in the main town of Coosa, Luna's men were afraid that the Indians would run away and take their food with them, leaving the Spaniards to starve. It would seem, then, that we can rule out Tristán de Luna's men as suspects, though not as decisively as we have ruled out Pardo's.

This process of elimination leaves us with a single suspect—the Hernando de Soto expedition. David Mathews has independently concluded that the people at the King site were killed and wounded by De Soto's men (see chapter 8). In particular, he concludes that they were killed and wounded on October 18, 1540, in the battle at Mabila. If our reconstruction of De Soto's route is accurate, Mabila was in Alabama in the vicinity of the lower Cahaba River, some 190 miles distant from the King site (DePratter, Hudson, and Smith 1985). The De Soto chroniclers make it clear that, although thousands of Indians were killed in the battle at Mabila, some escaped, and many of them were seriously wounded. The only ones specifically mentioned are those who were found dead when the Spaniards began reconnoitering the country around Mabila after the battle (Ranjel 1922:128). Clearly some of those who escaped with wounds could have survived and returned to the King site.

The problem with Mabila as the place where the King site people were attacked is that the dead would have lain unburied for a very long time indeed. The time for those who were killed within the town of Mabila would have differed from that for those who escaped to die of their wounds later. Traveling twenty miles per day, the Indians could have gone from Mabila to the King site in about ten days. Once the news of the battle reached people at the King site, it would have taken another ten days for them to have traveled to the vicinity of Mabila to retrieve the bodies and another ten days to carry them back to the King site. This is an elapsed time of thirty days. Even if we allow for faster travel—say seven days instead of ten—the bodies would still have been exposed for three weeks.

The bodies of those who were killed within the palisade at Mabila would have been exposed for an even longer period of time. After the battle ended, De Soto and his men remained in the vicinity of Mabila for about a month—from October 18 until November 14—while their wounds healed. During this time, they laid waste to the country, killing all who fell into their hands. Although the stench must have been terrible, there is no evidence that the Spaniards buried or otherwise disposed of the Indian corpses. It is not reasonable to think that people from the King site could have gone inside the town of Mabila to pick up the bodies of their dead until after De Soto and his men had departed. In short, the people of the King site would not have been able to retrieve bodies from inside the town until November 15, and they could not have returned to the King site with these bodies before about November 25. If the bodies at the King site were retrieved from within the palisade at Mabila, they would have lain unburied for about five and a half weeks.

Three to five and a half weeks is a long time for bodies to lie unburied. But there is good reason to think that the people of the King site would have retrieved the bodies of their dead kinsmen no matter how long they lay exposed. Even in the eighteenth century, the southeastern Indians hated for one of their number to die outside their homeland (Adair 1930:189). People from the King site could have carried the bodies home on stretchers, like those used by the Timucuans of coastal Florida in the sixteenth century.

We would like to propose an alternative hypothesis about where and when the killing and wounding occurred. The amount of fighting in which De Soto's men engaged varied from place to place. In the vicinity of present-day Tallahassee, the Indians of Apalachee bitterly contested De Soto and his army (figure 9.1). The people abandoned their towns and fled into the swamps and forests, from whence their warriors raided the Spaniards throughout the winter of 1539–1540. When De Soto's expedition began moving again, heading toward southeastern Georgia, the next chiefdom they encountered, Capachequi, resisted as Apalachee had. But once they reached the fall-line region, the Indians no longer resisted. As De Soto's men traveled through the fall-line region toward the Northeast, visiting chiefdom after chiefdom, they were given peaceful welcomes (Hudson, Smith, and DePratter 1985).

The first stirrings of resistance began when De Soto crossed the Blue Ridge Mountains and entered the northern end of the paramount chiefdom of Coosa (DePratter, Hudson, and Smith 1985). The first town was Chiaha, which they reached on June 5, 1540. Here De Soto and his men rested until June 28. The Indians of Chiaha did not resist, but when De Soto ordered the chief to give him thirty women to be slaves, some of the men fled with their women and children. As punishment, De Soto's men destroyed the cornfields of some of those who had fled (Elvas 1968:71). In this way De Soto coerced the chief of Chiaha into supplying him with five hundred burden bearers (Ranjel 1922:108).

On July 9, De Soto arrived at Coste, which was on Bussell Island, in the mouth of the Little Tennessee River. When some of his infantry began rummaging through the Indians' houses, taking what they pleased, some of the Indians took offense. They took up their war clubs and attacked five or six of De Soto's men. But De Soto, by a clever stratagem, avoided all-out conflict. He managed to seize the chief of Coste along with ten or twelve of his principal men. He put them in chains and held them as hostages (Elvas 1968:73–74; Ranjel 1922:109–110). Then he threatened to burn them to death because the warriors of Coste had dared to strike Spaniards (Ranjel 1922:110).

De Soto and his men reached the main town of Coosa on July 16, and they remained there until August 20. While they were there, the Indians fled into the woods, but De Soto's soldiers went out and captured many men and women, putting them in chains (Ranjel 1922:112). Some of these slaves later escaped by filing off their chains at night. Others escaped with their chains (Elvas 1968:77).

After departing from Coosa they passed through Itaba (compare "Etowah") without incident, although they acquired a number of women and burden bearers there (Elvas 1968:85; Ranjel 1922:113). But when they reached Ulibahali on August 31, De Soto found the Indians armed and ready for combat in a heavily palisaded village. They were angry because De Soto had put the chief of Coosa in chains and was taking him along as a hostage. But the chief of Coosa persuaded the warriors of Ulibahali to lay down their arms. Then they supplied De Soto with twenty or thirty women as slaves and with burdeners to carry their supplies (Elvas 1968:78–79; Ranjel 1922:113).

De Soto departed from Ulibahali on September 2, reaching a small village on the bank of the Coosa River. The De Soto chroniclers do not name this village, but it was probably Apica, which as we have already seen was later visited by Luna's men. They remained at Apica for one night before continuing on to another small town, Piachi, which was probably at the King site (Oviedo 1959:171). Here Captain Johan Ruiz Lobillo left the camp without permission and backtracked in an attempt to capture a black slave of his who deserted the expedition while they were in Ulibahali. De Soto had to remain at Piachi for an extra day and night while Lobillo was absent. When Lobillo returned, De Soto was angry and castigated him severely (Ranjel 1922:114).

Lobillo's slave was not the only person who had left the expedition. The desertions began after De Soto departed from Cofitachequi, where some of his company wanted to stay and establish a colony (Elvas 1968:164–168). De Soto forced them to continue, and as they were going from Cofitachequi to Xuala, one of his soldiers deserted. Two others attempted to escape when the expedition was crossing the mountains. They left behind at Coosa a black man, Robles, who was crippled and unable to walk any farther. Perhaps emboldened by the abandonment of Robles, a Levantine named Falco Herrado deserted and remained behind at Coosa. At Ulibahali, Mançano, a native of Salamanca, Spain, either strayed and became lost, or else he, too, chose to remain behind (Elvas 1968:79). Such desperate acts could have been committed only by men who had come to see the De Soto expedition as unbearably oppressive or else as a hopeless failure.

Even though none of the De Soto chroniclers specifically mentions violence during the day and two nights they were at Piachi—probably the King site— clearly the Indians of Coosa were becoming more and more restive as De Soto traveled through their land. It is clear as well that the Indians sometimes fled their towns in an attempt to avoid enslavement and that the Spaniards sometimes went and captured them by force. Also, De Soto's men had to hold their slaves by force after gaining possession of them, and these people were far less accustomed to coerced labor than were the peasants whom the Spaniards found in the Valley of Mexico and in Peru. Furthermore, the series of desertions from the expedition at about this time suggests anger and estrangement among at least some of De Soto's own men.

Given such volatile conditions, the likelihood that Indians might be slaughtered by De Soto's men was great. The ones killed at the King site could have been Indians who resisted enslavement, or perhaps some of the people who had been enslaved revolted. It is also possible that the violence was touched off when the Spaniards extorted or stole food and supplies from the people at the King site. If the people at the King site fled into the woods to escape De Soto and his men, this could explain why the bodies were gnawed by rodents and other animals before they could be buried.

It is quite clear that De Soto was taking young women by force, and the Indians were angered by this practice. He first attempted it at Chiaha but apparently did not succeed (Elvas 1968:175–176). He obtained four women at Coste (Elvas 1968:81; Ranjel 1922:110); many men and women at Coosa (Elvas 1968:83; Ranjel 1922:112); thirty women at Itaba (Elvas 1968:85; Ranjel 1922:113); and twenty or thirty women at Ulibahali (Ranjel 1922:113). Later in the expedition, when De Soto reached Athahachi, one of the ploys that Tascaluza used to coax De Soto to Mabila was the promise of all the women he wanted. At Mabila, after a group of particularly attractive young women had danced for the Spaniards, Tascaluza launched a large-scale surprise attack against De Soto and his men.

We now have two possible scenarios for the violent deaths at the King site: in the battle at Mabila or in and around the King site. The former has the advantage of being a well-documented battle that was described by all of the De Soto chroniclers. None of the chroniclers mentions a military action against the Indians at the King site. But the mere fact that no killings or woundings are mentioned as having taken place at the King site does not mean that none occurred. A close reading of the De Soto narratives shows that matters which became routine ceased to be mentioned by the chroniclers. By the time De Soto reached the King site, the enslavement of women, the impressment of both sexes into service as burdeners, and the killing of Indians may all have been routine.

It is possible that further research on the skeletal remains of the victims could rule out one of the two possibilities. If the victims were killed in the vicinity of the King site, they would have lain unburied only a few days and not three to five weeks or more, as they would have if they had been killed at Mabila. A reliable means of measuring the amount of time the bodies were exposed would decide the case if one could be devised. The gnawed bones, for example, may contain unsuspected information. It would be reasonable to expect far more gnawing to have occurred if the bodies had been exposed in and around Mabila than if they had been exposed in and around the King site.

David Mathews uses the sex and age characteristics of the killed and wounded to support his argument that the battle took place at Mabila (1984b:70–71). Specifically, he argues that Mabila is the likely place because: (1) there are no children among the victims; (2) there is a high proportion of females under age twenty-five and a high proportion of both sexes over forty, suggesting that they were slaves and burdeners; and (3) there are few males under twenty-five, whereas one would have expected more young males to have been wounded and killed if a large military engagement had taken place at the King site. But this evidence of sex and age is ambiguous.

It is not surprising that no individuals under ten years of age were among the killed and wounded, since children were not ordinarily combatants. Ironically, however, the chroniclers do mention young children fighting and being killed at Mabila (Ranjel 1922:127). Moreover, the chroniclers mention that one of the things that initially made the Spaniards suspicious upon entering Mabila is that no children were to be seen (Garcilaso 1962:355). Hence the children who took part in the battle at Mabila were probably the children of the female slaves the Spaniards had brought with them.

The high proportion of females of age twenty to twenty-five is consistent with De Soto's practice of enslaving young females. But the high proportion of both sexes over fifty years of age (three females and six males) would not seem to be consistent with their use as burdeners. That is, it is far more likely that such old people were killed while trying to protect their younger relatives than that they were impressed into service as burdeners.

The absence of twenty- to twenty-five-year-old males among the killed and wounded is surprising. But nonetheless there are four males younger than thirty-five (as compared with six females), and all of them are of warrior age.

If the people of the King site were killed at Mabila, it is striking that none of them appears to have been wounded or killed by a halberd, a weapon that was definitely used by De Soto's soldiers at Mabila. Furthermore, none of the individuals shows evidence of having been burned, whereas many of the Indians at Mabila were burned to death in the houses. It is possible to explain this difficulty away by arguing that the Indians who were burned were unrecognizable and were therefore not carried back to the King site. One could also argue that the individuals at the King site who died of their wounds were those who escaped from Mabila and later died.

Neither of the two hypotheses explains why none of the dead and wounded show signs of having been attacked by the large war dogs that De Soto used (Varner and Varner 1983). De Soto began using these dogs against the Indians in Florida, and the survivors of the expedition were still using them in eastern Texas toward the end of the expedition. One would expect these dogs to have been used both in rounding up slaves and in punishing them, and they would most certainly have been used in an all-out attack.

In our process of elimination, we have thus far not considered yet another suspect—Indians who were enemies of the people at the King site. The strong palisades around Ulibahali and the King site indicate that the Indians of the upper Coosa River did have enemies at hand. Also, archaeological evidence has shown that the Indians of the chiefdom of Coosa obtained a few steel weapons in the sixteenth century. But even though the Indians possessed some steel weapons, it is impossible that they could have used them to inflict wounds identical in kind and frequency to those inflicted in episodes of medieval European warfare (see chapter 8). Moreover, the high proportion of female casualties suggests that Indians were not the perpetrators of the massacre. The southeastern Indians did occasionally kill women but more commonly captured them.

Even though we can rule out Indians as the perpetrators of the King site massacre, it is still possible that some of the injuries and deaths were caused by Indians. There is no lack of evidence of traumatic injury among precontact Mississippian populations (Lahren and Berryman 1984). Hence, De Soto's men may not have caused *all* of the injuries and deaths at the King site.

People clearly continued living at the King site after 1540. The site was almost certainly still occupied at the time of the Tristán de Luna expedition. But within another ten years, by about 1570, the village was abandoned. Many of the houses had burned. Some of these fires could have been accidental, and some of them could have been deliberately set in connection with funeral rites. Others could have been set by Indian enemies of the people at the King site. As De Soto was to learn during a bitter winter at Chicaça, the Indians were capable of using fire very effectively in attacks against their enemies.

The time has come to draw this investigation to a close. We know who committed the crime. And we know what kinds of weapons were used, though it is puzzling that some of the weapons that could have been used—halberds and dogs—appear not to have been used. There is some evidence from the Pardo expeditions that warriors from the chiefdom of Coosa may have fought in alliance with Tascaluza's warriors in the battle at Mabila (Hudson 1987, n.d.).

We do not know for certain where and when the people at the King site were injured and killed. The massacre could have occurred either at Mabila or at the King site. One hopes that the necessary clues are present in the skeletal remains and that Robert Blakely and David Mathews will develop clever new ways of discovering and interpreting them. But as it stands now, if Sherlock Holmes were summarizing the case to his faithful colleague and companion, he would no doubt say: "Whatever the King site case is, my dear Watson, it is not elementary."

Appendix

King Site Burials Analyzed

Burial number[a]	Sex[b]	Age (in years)[c]	Public/private[d]	Wounds[e]	Animal bite marks	Periosteal reactions
1	F	45–50	public	F	X	X
2-1	M	A	public			
2-2	I	0.5	public			
2-3	I	2	public			
3	F	35–40	public			
4	I	3	public			
5	F	35–40	public			
6-1	F	25–28	public			
6-2	M	45–50	public			
7	M	28–30	public			
9	F	60–70				
10	I	7–8				
12	I	3				
13	I	4–5				
14	F	A				
18-1	F	24–26				
18-2	I	3				
21	F	25–28				

(*continued*)

Burial number[a]	Sex[b]	Age (in years)[c]	Public/ private[d]	Wounds[e]	Animal bite marks	Periosteal reactions
22	F	21–25				
23	M	50–60		F		
24	M	50–60		H		X
25	F	40–45				
29	M	45–50				
30	M	45–50	public			
31	I	2–3	public			
32-1	I	A	public			
32-2	I	3–4	public			
33	I	3–4	public			
34	M	50–60	public	F	X	
37	F	A	public			
38	I	3	public			
39	F	25–28	public			
40	F	45–50	public			
42	M	A				
43	I	4				
44	M	35–40		H		X
45	F	21–25		F		
46	I	9–10				
47	I	4–5				
48	F	21–25			X	
49	M	45–50				
50	F(?)	13–14		F		
51	I	2				
52	I	7–8				
53	F	40–45		H		X
54-1	F	35–40		H	X	
54-2	M	25–28				
55	F	70+		F		
56	M	35–40			X	
57	M	25–28		H	X	X
58	I	5				
59	M	18–19		F		X
60	I	3				
61	I	3				
62	F	45–50		F	X	

(*continued*)

Burial number[a]	Sex[b]	Age (in years)[c]	Public/ private[d]	Wounds[e]	Animal bite marks	Periosteal reactions
63	M	17–18			X	X
64	I	7–8				
65	M	50–60			X	
66	F	21–22				
67	F	50–60				
68	I	3				
69	F	45–50				
70	F	A				
71	I	4				
72	I	A				
73-1	M	50–60			X	
73-2	F	15–16				
74	F	50–60	public	H		X
75	I	A				
76	F	45–50				
77	I	6				
78	I	6				
79	M	A				
80	I	5				
81	M	60–70				
82	F	20–21				
83	F	45–50		F	X	
84	M	40–50			X	X
85	M	30–40	public	H		
86	I	A	public			
87	F	21–25	public			
88	I	4–5				
89	F	21–25		F		
90	I	5				
91	I	1				
92	M	45–50		F		
93	M	16–17				
96	I	A				
97	F(?)	14–15				
98	I	A				
99	I	3	public			
100	M	45–50	public			

(*continued*)

Burial number[a]	Sex[b]	Age (in years)[c]	Public/ private[d]	Wounds[e]	Animal bite marks	Periosteal reactions
101	M	50–60	public			
102	M	50–60	public			
103	M	50–60	public	F		
104	M	45–50	public			
105	M	45–50	public			
106	I	20–30	public			
107	F(?)	12–13	public			
108	I	A	public			
109	M	50+	public			
110	I	3				
111	F	25–28				
113	F	25–28				
114	F	21–25				
116	I	A				
117	I	28–30	public(?)			
118	M	35–40	public(?)			
119	I	A				
120	F	18			X	
121	M	25–28		H		X
122	F	40–45		F		
123	F	45–50		F	X	
124	F	40–45		H		
125	I	4				
126	M	35–40		F	X	
128	F	45–50		F	X	
129	M	45–50			X	
130	M	50–60		F		
131	F	15–20				
132	F	30–40				
133	I	10–11				
135	F	40–45				
136	F	45–50				
138	F	40–45		F		
139	F	45–50				
140	M	45–50			X	
142	I	1.3				
144	F	30–35				
145	M	28–30				

(continued)

Burial number[a]	Sex[b]	Age (in years)[c]	Public/ private[d]	Wounds[e]	Animal bite marks	Periosteal reactions
146	M	50–60		H		X
147	I	A				
148	F	35–40			X	
149	F	40–45		F	X	
150	M	50–60		F		X
151	F	60–70				
152	I	4				
153	M	45–50		H		
154	I	3				
156	F	20–21				
157	F	16–17				
158	I	4				
160	I	5				
161	F	A				
162	F	35–40				
164	I	4				
165	M	30–40				
166	F	15–16				
167	I	9–10				
169	F	30–35				
170	I	8				
172	F	20–30				
174	I	A				
175	I	2				
176	F	25–28				
177	M	A				
178	I	2–3				
179	I	A				
181	F	18				
182	I	A				
184	I	3				
185	F	21–25		F	X	
186	F(?)	10–11				
187	F(?)	11–12				
188	F	21–25		F		
189	M	30–40				
190	I	A		F		
191	M	45–50				

(*continued*)

Burial number[a]	Sex[b]	Age (in years)[c]	Public/ private[d]	Wounds[e]	Animal bite marks	Periosteal reactions
192	F	40–50				
193	I	4				
194	I	A	public			
195	I	1				
196	F	20–21				
198	M	50–60		F		
201	I	8				
203	I	A				
209	I	2–3				
210	F	21–25				
211	F	40–45		F		
212	M	50–60				
215	I	A				
216	I	4				
217	I	A				
219	I	6				
220	M(?)	12–13				
221	F(?)	11–12				
Str. 5	M	45–50		F		
Str. 5-A	M	18				
Str. 5-B	F	50+				
Str. 5-C	F	60+				

[a]Because of poor preservation, not all burials contained recoverable bone; therefore there are gaps in the sequence of burial numbers.

[b]F = female. M = male. I = indeterminate.

[c]A = adult.

[d]Only public sector burials are indicated; the remainder are private. Public sector burials, which held high-status individuals, were located in the plaza and ceremonial structure. Private sector burials, which held low-status individuals, were located in and around domestic dwellings (see figure 2.1).

[e]F = fatal. H = healed.

References

Acsádi, György, and J. Nemeskéri. 1970. *History of Human Life Span and Mortality.* Budapest: Akadémiai Kiadó.

Adair, James. 1930. *Adair's History of the American Indians*, ed. Samuel Cole Williams. New York: Promontory Press.

Angel, J. Lawrence. 1969. Paleodemography and Evolution. *American Journal of Physical Anthropology* 31:343–353.

Armelagos, George J. 1969. Disease in Ancient Nubia. *Science* 163:255–259.

Asch, David L. 1976. *The Middle Woodland Population of the Lower Illinois Valley: A Study in Paleodemographic Methods.* Scientific Papers No. 1. Evanston: Northwestern University Archaeology Program.

Ashworth, Joel Thomas, Jr., Marvin Jerome Allison, Enrique Gerszten, and Alejandro Pezzia. 1976. The Pubic Scars of Gestation and Parturition in a Group of Pre-Columbian and Colonial Peruvian Mummies. *American Journal of Physical Anthropology* 45:85–89.

Bass, William M. 1971. *Human Osteology: A Laboratory and Field Manual of the Human Skeleton.* Columbia: Missouri Archaeological Society.

Beck, Lane A. 1985. Trace Elements and Dietary Variation During the Mississippian Period in North Georgia. Paper presented at the forty-second annual meeting of the Southeastern Archaeological Conference, Birmingham.

Berryman, Hugh E. 1980. Mouse Creek, Dallas, and Middle Cumberland: A Multivariate Approach. In *The Skeletal Biology of Aboriginal Populations in the Southeastern United States*, ed. Patrick S. Willey and Fred H. Smith, 1–14. Tennessee Anthropological Association, Miscellaneous Paper No. 5. Chattanooga: Tennessee Anthropological Association.

Binford, Lewis R. 1971. Mortuary Practices: Their Study and Their Potential. In *Approaches to the Social Dimensions of Mortuary Practices*, ed. James A. Brown, 6–29. Memoirs of the Society for American Archaeology, No. 25. Washington, D.C.: Society for American Archaeology.

Birkby, Walter H. 1966. An Evaluation of Race and Sex Identification from Cranial Measurements. *American Journal of Physical Anthropology* 24:21–28.

Black, Francis L. 1980. Modern Isolated Pre-agricultural Populations as a Source of Information on Prehistoric Epidemic Patterns. In *Changing Disease Patterns and Human Behavior*, ed. N. S. Stanley and R. A. Joske, 37–54. New York: Academic Press.

Blackith, R. E., and R. A. Reyment. 1971. *Multivariate Morphometrics*. New York: Academic Press.

Blakely, Robert L. 1971. Comparison of the Mortality Profiles of Archaic, Middle Woodland, and Middle Mississippian Skeletal Populations. *American Journal of Physical Anthropology* 34:43–54.

————. 1977. Sociocultural Implications of Demographic Data from Etowah, Georgia. In *Biocultural Adaptation in Prehistoric America*, ed. Robert L. Blakely, 45–66. Proceedings of the Southern Anthropological Society, No. 11. Athens: University of Georgia Press.

————. 1980. Sociocultural Implications of Pathology Between the Village Area and Mound C Skeletal Remains from Etowah, Georgia. In *The Skeletal Biology of Aboriginal Populations in the Southeastern United States*, ed. Patrick S. Willey and Fred H. Smith, 28–38. Tennessee Anthropological Association, Miscellaneous Paper No. 5. Chattanooga: Tennessee Anthropological Association.

————. 1984. Personal communication with John Garrett. 17 January.

Blakely, Robert L., and Lane A. Beck. 1981. Trace Elements, Nutritional Status, and Social Stratification at Etowah, Georgia. In *The Research Potential of Anthropological Museum Collections*, ed. Anne-Marie Cantwell, James B. Griffin, and Nan A. Rothschild, 417–431. New York: New York Academy of Sciences.

————. 1984. Tooth-Tool Use Versus Dental Mutilation: A Case

Study from the Prehistoric Southeast. *Midcontinental Journal of Archaeology* 9:269–284.

Blakely, Robert L., and Antoinette B. Brown. 1985. Functionally Adaptive Biocultural Diversity in the Coosa Chiefdom of Sixteenth-Century Georgia. Paper presented at the fifty-fourth annual meeting of the American Association of Physical Anthropologists, Knoxville.

Blakely, Robert L., and Bettina Detweiler-Blakely. 1985. The Impact of European Disease at the Sixteenth-Century King Site in Georgia. Paper presented at the eighty-fourth annual meeting of the American Anthropological Association, Washington, D.C.

————. 1987. Testing the Validity of Enamel Hypoplasias as Stress Indicators. Paper presented at the eighty-sixth annual meeting of the American Anthropological Association, Chicago.

Blakely, Robert L., and David S. Mathews. 1975. Demographic Model of the Etowah Village Population. *Bulletin of the Georgia Academy of Science* 33:168–179.

————. 1985. The Burials at 9Eb85. In *Archaeological Investigations at the Beaverdam Creek Site (9Eb85), Elbert County, Georgia*, ed. James L. Rudolph and David J. Hally, 317–351. Atlanta: Archaeological Services, Russell Papers, National Park Service.

Blalock, Hubert M. 1972. *Social Statistics.* New York: McGraw-Hill.

Bolton, Herbert E., and Mary Ross. 1925. *The Debatable Land.* Berkeley: University of California Press.

Boumans, P. W. J. M. 1978. Inductively Coupled Plasma–Atomic Emission Spectroscopy: Its Present and Future Position in Analytical Chemistry. *Optica Pura y Aplicada* 11:143–171.

Bourne, Edward Gaylord. 1904. *Narratives of the Career of Hernando de Soto.* 2 vols. New York: Allerton.

Brose, David S. 1972. Comment on "Tooth Wear and Culture: A Survey of Tooth Function Among Some Prehistoric Populations," by Stephen Molnar. *Current Anthropology* 13:517.

Broster, John B. 1972. The Ganier Site: A Late Mississippian Village on the Cumberland River. In *The Middle Cumberland Culture*, ed. Robert B. Ferguson, 51–78. Nashville: Vanderbilt University Press.

Brothwell, Don R. 1965. *Digging Up Bones.* London: British Museum of Natural History.

Brown, Antoinette B. 1973. *Bone Strontium Content as a Dietary Indicator in Human Skeletal Populations.* Ph.D. dissertation, University of Michigan. Ann Arbor: University Microfilms.

————. 1984. Cortical Bone Growth of King Site Juveniles. Paper presented at the nineteenth annual meeting of the Southern Anthropological Society, Atlanta.

Brown, Antoinette B., and Robert L. Blakely. 1985. Biocultural Adaptation as Reflected in Trace Element Distribution. *Journal of Human Evolution* 14:461–468.

Brown, James A., ed. 1971. *Approaches to the Social Dimensions of Mortuary Practices.* Memoirs of the Society for American Archaeology, No. 25. Washington, D.C.: Society for American Archaeology.

————. 1976. The Southern Cult Reconsidered. *Midcontinental Journal of Archaeology* 1:115–135.

Buikstra, Jane E. 1972. *Hopewell in the Lower Illinois River Valley: A Regional Approach to the Study of Biological Variability and Mortuary Activity.* Ph.D. dissertation, University of Chicago. Ann Arbor: University Microfilms.

————. 1977. Biocultural Dimensions of Archeological Study: A Regional Perspective. In *Biocultural Adaptation in Prehistoric America,* ed. Robert L. Blakely, 67–84. Proceedings of the Southern Anthropological Society, No. 11. Athens: University of Georgia Press.

Buikstra, Jane E., and Della Collins Cook. 1980. Palaeopathology: An American Account. *Annual Review of Anthropology* 9:433–470.

Buikstra, Jane E., and James H. Mielke. 1985. Demography, Diet, and Health. In *The Analysis of Prehistoric Diets,* ed. Robert I. Gilbert, Jr., and James H. Mielke, 359–422. New York: Academic Press.

Burnet, Macfarlane, and David O. White. 1972. *Natural History of Infectious Disease.* 4th ed. Cambridge: Cambridge University Press.

Caldwell, Joseph R. 1958. *Trend and Tradition in the Prehistory of the Eastern United States.* American Anthropological Association, Memoir 88. Washington, D.C.: American Anthropological Association.

Cassidy, Claire Monod. 1972. *A Comparison of Nutrition and Health in Pre-Agricultural and Agricultural Amerindian Skeletal Populations.* Ph.D. dissertation, University of Wisconsin—Madison. Ann Arbor: University Microfilms.

————. 1984. Skeletal Evidence for Prehistoric Subsistence Adaptation in the Central Ohio River Valley. In *Paleopathology at the Origins of Agriculture,* ed. Mark Nathan Cohen and George J. Armelagos, 307–345. New York: Academic Press.

Clarke, Steven K. 1978. *Markers of Metabolic Insult: The Association of Radiopaque Transverse Lines, Enamel Hypoplasias, and Enamel Histopathologies in a Prehistoric Skeletal Sample.* Ph.D. dissertation, University of Colorado. Ann Arbor: University Microfilms.

Cohen, Mark Nathan, and George J. Armelagos, eds. 1984. *Paleopathology at the Origins of Agriculture.* New York: Academic Press.

Cook, Della Collins. 1984. Subsistence and Health in the Lower Illinois Valley: Osteological Evidence. In *Paleopathology at the Origins of Agriculture,* ed. Mark Nathan Cohen and George J. Armelagos, 235–269. New York: Academic Press.

Corruccini, Robert S. 1974. An Examination of the Meaning of Cranial Discrete Traits for Human Skeletal Biological Studies. *American Journal of Physical Anthropology* 40:425–446.

Creamer, Winifred, and Jonathan Haas. 1985. Tribe Versus Chiefdom in Lower Central America. *American Antiquity* 50:738–754.

Crouch, James E. 1965. *Functional Human Anatomy.* Philadelphia: Lea and Febiger.

Crowder, Lisa E. 1985. Personal communication with Sharon Kestle. 5 January.

Dahlberg, Albert A., and Renée M. Menegaz-Bock. 1958. Emergence of the Permanent Teeth in Pima Indian Children: A Critical Analysis of Method and an Estimate of Population Parameters. *Journal of Dental Research* 37:1123–1140.

DePratter, Chester. 1983. *Late Prehistoric and Early Historic Chiefdoms in the Southeastern United States.* Ph.D. dissertation, University of Georgia. Ann Arbor: University Microfilms.

DePratter, Chester, Charles Hudson, and Marvin Smith. 1983. Juan Pardo's Explorations in the Interior Southeast, 1566–1568. *The Florida Historical Quarterly* 62:125–158.

———. 1985. The Hernando de Soto Expedition: From Chiaha to Mabila. In *Alabama and Its Borderlands, from Prehistory to Statehood,* ed. Reid R. Badger and Lawrence A. Clayton, 108–126. University: University of Alabama Press.

Detweiler-Blakely, Bettina. 1984. Periostitis as a Stress Indicator at the King Site in Georgia. Paper presented at the nineteenth annual meeting of the Southern Anthropological Society, Atlanta.

———. 1985. Personal communication with Robert Blakely. 6 October.

Driver, Harold E. 1961. *Indians of North America.* Chicago: University of Chicago Press.

Elias, Michael. 1980. The Feasibility of Dental Strontium Analysis for Diet-Assessment of Human Populations. *American Journal of Physical Anthropology* 53:1–4.

El-Najjar, Mahmoud Y., Mike V. DeSanti, and Leon Ozebek. 1978. Prevalence and Possible Etiology of Dental Enamel Hypoplasias. *American Journal of Physical Anthropology* 48:185–192.

Elvas, Gentleman of. 1968. Narrative. In *Narratives of De Soto in the Conquest of Florida*, trans. Buckingham Smith. Gainesville, Fla.: Palmetto Books.

Ericksen, Mary Frances. 1976. Cortical Bone Loss with Age in Three Native American Populations. *American Journal of Physical Anthropology* 45:443–452.

Ferguson, Robert B. 1972. The Arnold Village Site Excavations of 1965–1966. In *The Middle Cumberland Culture*, ed. Robert B. Ferguson, 1–49. Nashville: Vanderbilt University Press.

Folmsbee, Stanley J., and Madeline Kneberg Lewis, eds. 1965. Journals of the Juan Pardo Expeditions, 1566–1567. *East Tennessee Historical Society's Publications* 37:106–121.

Funkhouser, Gary. 1978. Paleodemography of the King Site. M.A. thesis, University of Georgia, Athens.

Garcilaso de la Vega. 1962. *The Florida of the Inca*. Austin: University of Texas Press.

Garn, Stanley M. 1966. Malnutrition and Skeletal Development in the Pre-School Child. In *Pre-School Child Malnutrition*, 43–62. Washington, D.C.: National Academy of Sciences, National Research Council.

————. 1970. *The Earlier Gain and Later Loss of Cortical Bone*. Springfield, Ill.: Charles C Thomas.

————. 1972. The Course of Bone Gain and the Phases of Bone Loss. *Orthopedic Clinics of North America* 3:503–520.

Garn, Stanley M., C. G. Rohmann, M. Behar, F. Viteri, and M. A. Guzmán. 1964. Compact Bone Deficiency in Protein-Calorie Malnutrition. *Science* 145:1444–1445.

Garrett, John R. 1984. Artificial Cranial Deformation at the King Site. Paper presented at the nineteenth annual meeting of the Southern Anthropological Society, Atlanta.

Garrow, Patrick H. 1975. The Mouse Creek "Focus": A Reevaluation. *Southeastern Archaeological Conference Bulletin* 18:76–85.

————. 1984. Personal communication with Robert Blakely. 20 March.

Garrow, Patrick H., and Marvin T. Smith. 1973. The King Site (9Fi-5) Excavations, April 1971 Through August 1973: Collected Papers. Unpublished manuscript, University of Georgia, Athens.

Garruto, Ralph M. 1981. Disease Patterns of Isolated Groups. In *Biocultural Aspects of Disease*, ed. H. R. Rothchild, 557–593. New York: Academic Press.

Geidel, Richard A. 1982. Trace Element Studies for Mississippian Skeletal Remains: Findings from Neutron Activation Analysis. *Museum of Applied Science Center for Archaeology Journal* 2:13–16.

Gibson, Jon L. 1974. Aboriginal Warfare in the Southeast: An Alternative Perspective. *American Antiquity* 39:130–133.

Gilbert, B. Miles, and Thomas W. McKern. 1973. A Method for Aging the Female Os Pubis. *American Journal of Physical Anthropology* 38:31–38.

Gilbert, Robert I., Jr. 1975. *Trace Element Analyses of Three Skeletal Amerindian Populations at Dickson Mounds.* Ph.D. dissertation, University of Massachusetts, Amherst. Ann Arbor: University Microfilms.

————. 1977. Applications of Trace Element Research to Problems in Archeology. In *Biocultural Adaptation in Prehistoric America,* ed. Robert L. Blakely, 85–100. Proceedings of the Southern Anthropological Society, No. 11. Athens: University of Georgia Press.

————. 1985. Stress, Paleonutrition, and Trace Elements. In *The Analysis of Prehistoric Diets,* ed. Robert I. Gilbert, Jr., and James H. Mielke, 339–358. New York: Academic Press.

Goldman, Irving. 1970. *Ancient Polynesian Society.* Chicago: University of Chicago Press.

Goldstein, Lynne G. 1980. *Mississippian Mortuary Practices: A Case Study of Two Cemeteries in the Lower Illinois Valley.* Scientific Papers No. 2. Evanston: Northwestern University Archaeology Program.

Goodman, Alan H., George J. Armelagos, and Jerome C. Rose. 1980. Enamel Hypoplasias as Indicators of Stress in Three Indian Populations from Illinois. *Human Biology* 52:515–528.

Goodman, Alan H., Debra L. Martin, George J. Armelagos, and George Clark. 1984. Indicators of Stress from Bone and Teeth. In *Paleopathology at the Origins of Agriculture,* ed. Mark Nathan Cohen and George J. Armelagos, 13–49. New York: Academic Press.

Gordon, Claire C., and Jane E. Buikstra. 1981. Soil pH, Bone Preservation, and Sampling Bias at Mortuary Sites. *American Antiquity* 46:566–571.

Gould, Richard A. 1968. Chipping Stone in the Outback. *Natural History* 77:42–49.

Hally, David J. 1970. *Archaeological Investigations of the Potts Tract Site (9 Mu 103), Carters Dam, Murray County, Georgia.* Laboratory of Archaeology Series, Report No. 6. Athens: University of Georgia.

————. 1975a. Archaeological Investigations of the King Site,

Floyd County, Georgia. Manuscript on file, Department of Anthropology, University of Georgia, Athens.

———. 1975b. The King Site and Its Investigation. *Southeastern Archaeological Conference Bulletin* 18:48–54.

———. 1975c. Archaeological Investigation of the King Site. Final report submitted to the National Endowment for the Humanities.

———. 1979. *Archaeological Investigation of the Little Egypt Site (9 Mu 102), Murray County, Georgia, 1969 Season.* Laboratory of Archaeology Series, Report No. 18. Athens: University of Georgia.

———. 1986. An Overview of Lamar Culture. Paper presented at the fiftieth anniversary conference of the Ocmulgee National Monument, Macon, Ga.

Hally, David J., Patrick H. Garrow, and Wyman Trotti. 1975. Preliminary Analysis of the King Site Settlement Plan. *Southeastern Archaeological Conference Bulletin* 18:55–62.

Hamilton, M. E. 1975. *Variation Among Five Groups of Amerindians in the Magnitude of Sexual Dimorphism of Skeletal Size.* Ph.D. dissertation, University of Michigan. Ann Arbor: University Microfilms.

Harrold, Francis B. 1980. A Comparative Analysis of Eurasian Paleolithic Burials. *World Archaeology* 12:195–211.

Hatch, James W. 1976. *Status in Death: Principles of Ranking in Dallas Culture Mortuary Remains.* Ph.D. dissertation, Pennsylvania State University. Ann Arbor: University Microfilms.

Hatch, James W., and Richard A. Geidel. 1983. Tracing Status and Diet in Prehistoric Tennessee. *Archaeology* 36:56–59.

Hatch, James W., and Patrick S. Willey. 1974. Stature and Status in Dallas Society. *Tennessee Archaeologist* 30:107–131.

Hatch, James W., Patrick S. Willey, and Edward E. Hunt, Jr. 1983. Indicators of Status-Related Stress in Dallas Society: Transverse Lines and Cortical Thickness in Long Bones. *Midcontinental Journal of Archaeology* 8:49–71.

Haviland, William A. 1967. Stature at Tikal, Guatemala: Implications for Ancient Maya Demography and Social Organization. *American Antiquity* 32:316–325.

Hinton, Robert J. 1981. Form and Patterning of Anterior Tooth Wear Among Aboriginal Human Groups. *American Journal of Physical Anthropology* 54:555–564.

Hoffman, J. Michael. 1979. Age Estimations from Diaphyseal Lengths: Two Months to Twelve Years. *Journal of Forensic Sciences* 24:461–469.

Houghton, Philip. 1974. The Relationship of the Pre-auricular Groove of the Ilium to Pregnancy. *American Journal of Physical Anthropology* 41:381–389.

Howell, Nancy. 1976. Toward a Uniformitarian Theory of Human Paleodemography. In *The Demographic Evolution of Human Populations*, ed. R. H. Ward and Kenneth M. Weiss, 25–40. New York: Academic Press.

Hrdlička, Aleš. 1905. Head Deformation Among the Klamath, Maricopa Weaving, a Cora Cradle, and Jay Feathers in Cora Ceremony. *American Anthropologist* 7:360–362.

Hudson, Charles. 1976. *The Southeastern Indians.* Knoxville: University of Tennessee Press.

———. 1987. Juan Pardo's Excursion Beyond Chiaha. *Tennessee Anthropologist* 12:74–87.

———. In press. A Spanish-Coosa Alliance in Sixteenth-Century North Georgia.

Hudson, Charles, Marvin Smith, and Chester DePratter. 1985. The Hernando de Soto Expedition: From Apalachee to Chiaha. *Southeastern Archaeology* 3:65–77.

Hudson, Charles, Marvin Smith, David J. Hally, Richard Polhemus, and Chester DePratter. 1985. Coosa: A Chiefdom in the Sixteenth-Century Southeastern United States. *American Antiquity* 50:723–737.

———. 1987. Reply to Boyd and Schroedl [on the Reconstruction of the Coosa Chiefdom]. *American Antiquity* 52:845–856.

Imbelloni, José. 1950. Cephalic Deformations of the Indians in Argentina. *Bulletin of the Bureau of American Ethnology* 143:53–55. Washington, D.C.: Government Printing Office.

Johansson, S. Ryan, and S. Horowitz. 1986. Estimating Mortality in Skeletal Populations: Influence of the Growth Rate in the Interpretation of Levels and Trends During the Transition to Agriculture. *American Journal of Physical Anthropology* 71:233–250.

Johnston, Francis E. 1969. Approaches to the Study of Developmental Variability in Human Skeletal Populations. *American Journal of Physical Anthropology* 31:335–341.

Jurmain, Robert D. 1977. Stress and Etiology of Osteoarthritis. *American Journal of Physical Anthropology* 46:353–365.

Kelly, Arthur R., and Lewis H. Larson. 1957. Explorations at Etowah, Georgia, 1954–1956. *Archaeology* 10:39–48.

Kestle, Sharon. 1984. Dental Attrition and Sexual Division of Labor at the King Site. Paper presented at the nineteenth annual meeting of the Southern Anthropological Society, Atlanta.

Kroeber, Alfred L. 1963. *Cultural and Natural Areas of Native North America.* Berkeley: University of California Press.

Krogman, Wilton M. 1962. *The Human Skeleton in Forensic Medicine.* Springfield, Ill.: Charles C Thomas.

Lahren, Craig H., and Hugh E. Berryman. 1984. Fracture Patterns and Status at Chucalissa (40Syl): A Biocultural Approach. *Tennessee Anthropologist* 9:15–21.

Lallo, John, George J. Armelagos, and Jerome C. Rose. 1978. Paleoepidemiology of Infectious Disease in the Dickson Mounds Population. *Medical College of Virginia Quarterly* 14:17–23.

Lallo, John, and John E. Blank. 1977. Ancient Disease in Ohio: The Eiden Population. *Ohio Journal of Science* 77:55–62.

Larsen, Clark Spencer. 1981. Functional Implications of Postcranial Size Reduction on the Prehistoric Georgia Coast. *Journal of Human Evolution* 10:489–502.

————. 1982. *The Anthropology of St. Catherines Island, 3: Prehistoric Human Biological Adaptation.* Anthropological Papers, vol. 57, pt. 3. New York: American Museum of Natural History.

————. 1984. Health and Disease in Prehistoric Georgia: The Transition to Agriculture. In *Paleopathology at the Origins of Agriculture*, ed. Mark Nathan Cohen and George J. Armelagos, 367–392. New York: Academic Press.

Larson, Lewis H. 1971. Archaeological Implications of Social Stratification at the Etowah Site, Georgia. In *Approaches to the Social Dimensions of Mortuary Practices*, ed. James A. Brown, 58–67. Memoirs of the Society for American Archaeology, No. 25. Washington, D.C.: Society for American Archaeology.

————. 1972. Functional Considerations of Warfare in the Southeast During the Mississippi Period. *American Antiquity* 37:383–392.

Le Moyne de Morgues, Jacques. 1965. The Narrative of Jacques le Moyne de Morgues. In *The New World*, ed. Stefan Lorant, 33–86. New York: Duell, Sloan and Pearce.

Lewis, Thomas M. N., and Madeline Kneberg. 1946. *Hiwassee Island: An Archaeological Account of Four Tennessee Indian Peoples.* Knoxville: University of Tennessee Press.

————. 1955. *The First Tennesseans: An Interpretation of Tennessee Prehistory.* Department of Anthropology Papers. Knoxville: University of Tennessee.

Lowery, Woodbury. 1901. *The Spanish Settlements Within the Present Limits of the United States, 1513–1561.* New York: G. P. Putnam's Sons.

————. 1959. *The Spanish Settlements Within the Present Lim-*

its of the United States, 1562–1574. New York: Russell and Russell.

McKern, Thomas W., and T. Dale Stewart. 1957. *Skeletal Age Changes in Young American Males Analyzed from the Standpoint of Identification.* Headquarters Quartermaster Research and Development Command, Technical Report EP-45. Natick, Mass.

Massler, M., Isaac Schour, and H. G. Poncher. 1941. Developmental Pattern of the Child as Reflected in the Calcification Pattern of the Teeth. *American Journal of Diseases of Children* 62:33–67.

Mathews, David S. 1984a. Evidence of an Early Indian/Explorer Party Battle in Georgia. Paper presented at the nineteenth annual meeting of the Southern Anthropological Society, Atlanta.

——. 1984b. De Soto's Battle of Mabila: The Ulibahali Casualties from the King Site. M.A. thesis, Georgia State University, Atlanta.

Merchant, Virginia L., and Douglas H. Ubelaker. 1977. Skeletal Growth of the Protohistoric Arikara. *American Journal of Physical Anthropology* 46:61–72.

Molnar, Stephen. 1971. Human Tooth Wear, Tooth Function, and Cultural Variability. *American Journal of Physical Anthropology* 34:175–188.

Moorehead, Warren K. 1932. *Etowah Papers.* New Haven: Yale University Press.

Moorrees, Coenraad F. A., Elizabeth A. Fanning, and Edward E. Hunt, Jr. 1963a. Formation and Resorption of Three Deciduous Teeth in Children. *American Journal of Physical Anthropology* 21:205–213.

——. 1963b. Age Variation of Formation Stages of Ten Permanent Teeth. *Journal of Dental Research* 42:1490–1502.

Mormann, J. E., and H. R. Muhlemann. 1981. Oral Starch Degradation and Its Influence on Acid Production in Human Dental Plaque. *Caries Research* 15:166–175.

Morse, Dan. 1969. *Ancient Disease in the Midwest.* Report of Investigations, No. 15. Springfield: Illinois State Museum.

Neumann, Georg K. 1942. Types of Artificial Cranial Deformation. *American Antiquity* 7:306–311.

Neumann, Georg K., and Cheryl Gruber Waldman. 1968. Regression Formulae for the Reconstruction of the Stature of Hopewellian and Middle Mississippi Amerindian Populations. *Proceedings of the Indiana Academy of Science for 1967* 77:98–101.

Norr, Lynette. 1984. Prehistoric Subsistence and Health Status of Coastal Peoples from the Panamanian Isthmus of Lower Central America. In *Paleopathology at the Origins of Agriculture,* ed.

Mark Nathan Cohen and George J. Armelagos, 463–490. New York: Academic Press.

Oates, Karen. 1987. Personal communication with Robert Blakely. 24 August.

Ortner, Donald J. 1979. Disease and Mortality in the Early Bronze Age People of Bab edh-Dhra, Jordan. *American Journal of Physical Anthropology* 51:589–598.

Ortner, Donald J., and Walter G. T. Putschar. 1981. *Identification of Pathological Conditions in Human Skeletal Remains.* Washington, D.C.: Smithsonian Institution Press.

Oviedo, Gonzalo Fernandez de. 1959. *Historia General y Natural de las Indias.* Madrid: Ediciones Atlas.

Owsley, Douglas W., and Bryan L. Guevin. 1982. Cranial Deformation: A Cultural Practice of the Eighteenth-Century Overhill Cherokee. *Journal of Cherokee Studies* Fall 1982:79–81.

Palkovich, Ann M. 1978. *A Model of the Dimensions of Mortality and Its Application to Paleodemography.* Ph.D. dissertation, Northwestern University. Ann Arbor: University Microfilms.

Peebles, Christopher S. 1974. *Moundville: The Organization of a Prehistoric Community and Culture.* Ph.D. dissertation, University of California, Santa Barbara. Ann Arbor: University Microfilms.

————. 1977. Biocultural Adaptation in Prehistoric America: An Archeologist's Perspective. In *Biocultural Adaptation in Prehistoric America,* ed. Robert L. Blakely, 115–130. Proceedings of the Southern Anthropological Society, No. 11. Athens: University of Georgia Press.

————. 1983. Moundville: Late Prehistoric Sociopolitical Organization in the Southeastern United States. In *The Development of Political Organization in Native North America,* ed. Elisabeth Tooker, 183–198. 1979 Proceedings of the American Ethnological Society. Washington, D.C.: American Ethnological Society.

Peebles, Christopher S., and Susan M. Kus. 1977. Some Archaeological Correlates of Ranked Societies. *American Antiquity* 42:421–447.

Perzigian, Anthony J., Patricia A. Tench, and Donna J. Braun. 1984. Prehistoric Health in the Ohio River Valley. In *Paleopathology at the Origins of Agriculture,* ed. Mark Nathan Cohen and George J. Armelagos, 347–366. New York: Academic Press.

Phenice, T. W. 1969. A Newly Developed Visual Method of Sexing the Os Pubis. *American Journal of Physical Anthropology* 30:297–302.

Pindborg, J. J. 1970. *Pathology of the Dental Hard Tissues.* Philadelphia: W. B. Saunders.

Polhemus, Richard. 1985. Mississippian Architecture: Temporal, Technological, and Spatial Patterns of Structures at the Toqua Site (40MR6). M.A. thesis, University of Tennessee, Knoxville.

Powell, Mary Lucas. 1985. The Analysis of Dental Wear and Caries for Dietary Reconstruction. In *The Analysis of Prehistoric Diets,* ed. Robert I. Gilbert, Jr., and James H. Mielke, 307–338. New York: Academic Press.

Price, T. Douglas, and Maureen Kavanagh. 1982. Bone Composition and the Reconstruction of Diet: Examples from the Midwestern United States. *Midcontinental Journal of Archaeology* 7:61–79.

Priestly, Herbert Ingram. 1928. *The Luna Papers: Documents Relating to the Expedition of Don Tristán de Luna y Arellano for the Conquest of La Florida in 1559–1561.* 2 vols. Deland: Florida State Historical Society.

————. 1936. *Tristán de Luna: Conquistador of the Old South.* Philadelphia: Porcupine Press.

Quinn, David. 1977. *North America from Earliest Discovery to the First Settlements: The Norse Voyages to 1612.* New York: Harper and Row.

————, ed. 1979. *New American World: A Documentary History of North America to 1612.* Vol. 5. New York: Arno Press.

Ranjel, Rodrigo. 1922. Narrative. In *Narratives of the Career of Hernando de Soto,* ed. Edward G. Bourne, 43–150. New York: Allerton.

Robbins, Louise M. 1977. The Story of Life Revealed by the Dead. In *Biocultural Adaptation in Prehistoric America,* ed. Robert L. Blakely, 10–26. Proceedings of the Southern Anthropological Society, No. 11. Athens: University of Georgia Press.

Romero, Javier. 1970. Dental Mutilation, Trephination, and Cranial Deformation. In *Handbook of Middle American Indians,* vol. 9, ed. T. Dale Stewart, 50–67. Austin: University of Texas Press.

Rose, Jerome C., Barbara A. Burnett, Michael S. Nassaney, and Mark W. Blaeuer. 1984. Paleopathology and the Origins of Maize Agriculture in the Lower Mississippi Valley and Caddoan Culture Areas. In *Paleopathology at the Origins of Agriculture,* ed. Mark Nathan Cohen and George J. Armelagos, 393–424. New York: Academic Press.

Rose, Jerome C., Keith W. Condon, and Alan H. Goodman. 1985. Diet and Dentition: Developmental Disturbances. In *The Analy-*

sis of Prehistoric Diets, ed. Robert I. Gilbert, Jr., and James H. Mielke, 281–305. New York: Academic Press.

Rothschild, Nan A. 1975. Age and Sex, Status and Role, in Prehistoric Societies of Eastern North America. Ph.D. dissertation, New York University. Ann Arbor: University Microfilms.

Ruff, Christopher B., and Henry H. Jones. 1981. Bilateral Asymmetry in Cortical Bone of the Humerus and Tibia: Sex and Age Factors. Human Biology 53:69–86.

Ruff, Christopher B., Clark Spencer Larsen, and Wilson C. Hayes. 1984. Structural Changes in the Femur with the Transition to Agriculture on the Georgia Coast. American Journal of Physical Anthropology 64:125–136.

St. Hoyme, Lucile E., and William M. Bass. 1962. Human Skeletal Remains from Tollifero (Ha6) and Clarksville (Me14) Sites, John H. Kerr Reservoir Basin, Virginia. Bureau of American Ethnology, Bulletin 182:329–400. Washington, D.C.: Government Printing Office.

Sattenspiel, Lisa, and Henry Harpending. 1983. Stable Populations and Skeletal Age. American Antiquity 48:489–498.

Saxe, Arthur A. 1970. Social Dimensions of Mortuary Practices. Ph.D. dissertation, University of Michigan. Ann Arbor: University Microfilms.

Schoeninger, Margaret J. 1979. Diet and Status at Chalcatzingo: Some Empirical and Technical Aspects of Strontium Analysis. American Journal of Physical Anthropology 51:295–310.

————. 1982. Diet and the Evolution of the Modern Human Form in the Middle East. American Journal of Physical Anthropology 58:37–52.

Schoeninger, Margaret J., and Christopher S. Peebles. 1981. Some Notes on the Relationship Between Status and Diet at Moundville. Southeastern Archaeological Conference Bulletin 24:96–97.

Schour, Isaac, and M. Massler. 1944. Chart: Development of the Human Dentition. 2d ed. Chicago: American Dental Association.

Schour, Isaac, and Bernard G. Sarnat. 1942. Oral Manifestations of Occupational Origin. Journal of the American Medical Association 120:1197–1207.

Schroeder, Henry A., Isabel H. Tipton, and Alexis P. Nason. 1972. Trace Elements in Man: Strontium and Barium. Journal of Chronic Diseases 25:491–517.

Sears, William H. 1956. Excavation at Kolomoki, Final Report. Report No. 5, University of Georgia Series in Anthropology, Athens.

Seckinger, Ernest W. 1975. Preliminary Report on the Social Dimensions of the King Site Mortuary Practices. *Southeastern Archaeological Conference Bulletin* 18:67–73.

————. 1977. Social Complexity During the Mississippian Period in Northwest Georgia. M.A. thesis, University of Georgia, Athens.

Service, Elman R. 1962. *Primitive Social Organization, An Evolutionary Perspective.* New York: Random House.

Sillen, Andrew. 1981. Strontium and Diet at Hayonim Cave. *American Journal of Physical Anthropology* 56:131–137.

Sillen, Andrew, and Maureen Kavanagh. 1982. Strontium and Paleodietary Research. *Yearbook of Physical Anthropology* 25:67–90.

Singer, Ronald. 1953. Estimation of Age from Cranial Suture Closure. *Journal of Forensic Medicine* 1:52–59.

Smith, David M., Walter E. Nance, Ke Won Kang, Joe C. Christian, and C. Conrad Johnston, Jr. 1973. Genetic Factors in Determining Bone Mass. *Journal of Clinical Investigation* 52:2800–2808.

Smith, Marvin T. 1975. European Materials from the King Site. *Southeastern Archaeological Conference Bulletin* 18:63–66.

————. 1987. *Archaeology of Aboriginal Culture Change: Depopulation During the Early Historic Period.* Gainesville: University of Florida Press.

Smith, Patricia. 1972. Diet and Attrition in the Natufians. *American Journal of Physical Anthropology* 37:233–238.

Smith, Patricia, Ofer Bar-Yosef, and Andrew Sillen. 1984. Archaeological and Skeletal Evidence for Dietary Change During the Late Pleistocene/Early Holocene in the Levant. In *Paleopathology at the Origins of Agriculture,* ed. Mark Nathan Cohen and George J. Armelagos, 101–136. New York: Academic Press.

Steinbock, R. Ted. 1976. *Paleopathological Diagnosis and Interpretation: Bone Diseases in Ancient Human Populations.* Springfield, Ill.: Charles C Thomas.

Stewart, T. Dale. 1950. Deformity, Trephining, and Mutilation in South American Indian Skeletal Remains. *Bulletin of the Bureau of American Ethnology* 143:43–52. Washington, D.C.: Government Printing Office.

————. 1970. Identification of the Scars of Parturition in the Skeletal Remains of Females. In *Personal Identification in Mass Disasters,* ed. T. Dale Stewart, 127–133. Washington, D.C.: National Museum of Natural History.

————. 1973. *The People of America.* New York: Scribner's Sons.

Stewart, T. Dale, and Mildred Trotter, eds. 1954. *Basic Readings* on the Identification of Human Skeletons: Estimation of Age. New York: Wenner-Gren Foundation for Anthropological Research.

Suchey, Judy Myers. 1979. Problems in the Aging of Females Using the Os Pubis. *American Journal of Physical Anthropology* 51:467–470.

Suchey, Judy Myers, Dean V. Wiseley, Richard F. Green, and Thomas T. Noguchi. 1979. Analysis of Dorsal Pitting in the Os Pubis in an Extensive Sample of Modern American Females. *American Journal of Physical Anthropology* 51:517–540.

Sullivan, Lynne P. 1987. The Mouse Creek Phase Household. *Southeastern Archaeology* 6:16–29.

Swanton, John R. 1922. *Early History of the Creek Indians and Their Neighbors.* Bureau of American Ethnology Bulletin No. 73. Washington, D.C.: Government Printing Office.

―――. 1928. *Social Organization and Social Usages of the Indians of the Creek Confederacy.* Bureau of American Ethnology, Annual Report 42. Washington, D.C.: Government Printing Office.

―――. 1946. *Indians of the Southeastern United States.* Bureau of American Ethnology, Bulletin 137. Washington, D.C.: Government Printing Office.

Swedlund, Alan C., and George J. Armelagos. 1976. *Demographic Anthropology.* Dubuque, Iowa: W. C. Brown.

Szpunar, Carole Bryda, Joseph B. Lambert, and Jane E. Buikstra. 1978. Analysis of Excavated Bone by Atomic Absorption. *American Journal of Physical Anthropology* 48:199–202.

Tainter, Joseph. 1975. *The Archaeological Study of Social Change: Woodland Systems in West-Central Illinois.* Ph.D. dissertation, Northwestern University. Ann Arbor: University Microfilms.

Tally, Lucy. 1974. Demographic and Osteological Analysis of the King Site Population. Manuscript on file, Department of Anthropology, University of Georgia, Athens.

―――. 1975. Preliminary Analysis of the King Site Burial Population. *Southeastern Archaeological Conference Bulletin* 18:74–75.

Thieme, Frederick, and William J. Schull. 1957. Sex Determination from the Skeleton. *Human Biology* 29:242–273.

Thordeman, Bengt. 1939. *Armour from the Battle of Wisby 1361.* Uppsala: Almqvist and Wiksells Boktryckeri-A.-B.

Todd, T. W., and C. W. Lyon, Jr. 1925. Cranial Suture Closure. *American Journal of Physical Anthropology* 8:23–71.

Trinkaus, Erik. 1982. Artificial Cranial Deformation in the Shanidar 1 and 5 Neandertals. *Current Anthropology* 23:198–199.

Turner, Christy G., II. 1979. Dental Anthropological Indications of Agriculture Among the Jomon People of Japan. *American Journal of Physical Anthropology* 51:619–636.

Ubelaker, Douglas H. 1978. *Human Skeletal Remains*. Chicago: Aldine.

Ullrich, H. 1975. Estimation of Fertility by Means of Pregnancy and Childbirth Alterations at the Pubis, the Ilium, and the Sacrum. *Ossa* 2:23–39.

Underwood, Eric J. 1977. *Trace Elements in Human and Animal Nutrition*. 4th ed. New York: Academic Press.

Underwood, Jane H. 1979. *Human Variation and Human Microevolution*. Englewood Cliffs, N.J.: Prentice-Hall.

U.S. De Soto Commission. 1939. *Final Report of the United States De Soto Expedition Commission*. Washington, D.C.: Government Printing Office.

Vallois, Henri. 1960. Vital Statistics in Prehistoric Populations as Determined from Archaeological Data. In *The Application of Quantitative Methods in Archaeology*, ed. Robert F. Heizer and Sherburne F. Cook, 186–204. Chicago: Quadrangle.

Van Gerven, Dennis P., and George J. Armelagos. 1983. "Farewell to Paleodemography?" Rumors of Its Death Have Been Greatly Exaggerated. *Journal of Human Evolution* 12:353–360.

Varner, John G., and Jeannette J. Varner. 1951. *The Florida of the Inca*. Austin: University of Texas Press.

———. 1983. *Dogs of the Conquest*. Norman: University of Oklahoma Press.

Webb, William S. 1952. *The Jonathan Creek Village, Site 4, Marshall County, Kentucky*. Reports in Anthropology, No. 8. Lexington: University of Kentucky.

Weiss, Kenneth M. 1972. On the Systematic Bias in Skeletal Sexing. *American Journal of Physical Anthropology* 37:239–250.

———. 1973. *Demographic Models for Anthropology*. Memoirs of the Society for American Archaeology, No. 27. Washington D.C.: Society for American Archaeology.

———. 1975. Demographic Disturbance and the Use of Life Tables in Anthropology. In *Population Studies in Archaeology and Biological Anthropology: A Symposium*, ed. Alan C. Swedlund, 46–56. Memoirs of the Society for American Archaeology, No. 30. Washington, D.C.: Society for American Archaeology.

———. 1976. Demographic Theory and Anthropological Inference. *Annual Review of Anthropology* 5:351–381.

Wells, Calvin. 1964. *Bones, Bodies, and Disease.* New York: Praeger.

Williams, Samuel Cole, ed. 1930. *Adair's History of the American Indians.* Johnson City, Tenn.: Watauga Press.

Wilson, Daniel. 1862. *Prehistoric Man.* Vol. 2. London: Macmillan.

Wing, Elizabeth S., and Antoinette B. Brown. 1979. *Paleonutrition: Method and Theory in Prehistoric Foodways.* New York: Academic Press.

Zimmerman, Michael R., and Marc A. Kelley. 1982. *Atlas of Human Paleopathology.* New York: Praeger.

Živanović, Srboljub. 1982. *Ancient Diseases*, trans. Lovett F. Edwards. New York: Pica Press.

Contributors

Robert L. Blakely is an associate professor of anthropology at Georgia State University in Atlanta. He received his Ph.D. degree in anthropology from Indiana University. With grants from the National Science Foundation, Blakely has conducted bio-archaeological research on skeletons from the Etowah site, Oakland Cemetery in Atlanta, and the King site. He edited *Biocultural Adaptation in Prehistoric America* (University of Georgia Press, 1977) and is publishing with Bettina Detweiler-Blakely "The Impact of European Disease at the Sixteenth-Century King Site in Georgia." His areas of expertise include paleodemography, paleoepidemiology, paleonutrition, and forensic anthropology.

Antoinette B. Brown earned her doctorate in anthropology from the University of Michigan in 1973. A nutritional anthropologist, she was a pioneer in the use of trace element analyses to reconstruct diet and status in prehistoric skeletal populations. She is coauthor with Elizabeth Wing of *Paleonutrition: Method and Theory in Prehistoric Foodways* (Academic Press, 1979). Brown has also carried out nutritional research among contemporary peoples in Mexico, Africa, and the United States. She currently lives in Rockville, Maryland.

Lisa E. Crowder received her B.A. degree in anthropology from Georgia State University after completing an honors thesis entitled "Kinship and Social Organization at the Sixteenth-Century King Site in Georgia." She is preparing to enter a doctoral program in East Asian and Oceanic Studies. Crowder's interests include chiefdom-level social organization, kinship, and sociolinguistics.

Chester DePratter is an adjunct professor and research associate at the South Carolina Institute of Archaeology and Anthropology. He received his Ph.D. degree in anthropology from the University of Georgia in 1983. DePratter is coauthor with Hudson, Smith, Hally, and Polhemus of "Coosa: A Chiefdom in the Sixteenth-Century Southeastern United States" (*American Antiquity* 50:723–737). His areas of expertise include prehistoric archaeology, ethnohistory, and geoarchaeology of the southeastern United States.

Bettina Detweiler-Blakely holds a B.A. degree with honors in anthropology from Georgia State University. She intends to pursue graduate work in biological anthropology. With Blakely she is coauthoring "The Impact of European Disease at the Sixteenth-Century King Site in Georgia" and copresented a paper entitled "The King Site Before, During, and After the Spanish Encounter: A Bioarchaeological View." Detweiler-Blakely carried out the lion's share of the laboratory research on the King site skeletal remains. Her interests include dental anthropology, paleopathology, and biomedical anthropology.

John Garrett, when he completes his undergraduate degree in anthropology at the University of Nevada at Reno, plans to enter a graduate program in archaeology. After working for Garrow and Associates, Inc., an archaeological firm in Atlanta, he accepted a position at the Desert Research Institute in Reno. Garrett's research interests include geoarchaeology and bioarchaeology in the American Southwest.

David J. Hally is an associate professor of anthropology at the University of Georgia in Athens. He received his doctorate from Harvard University in 1972. With funds from the National Geographic Society, National Science Foundation, and National Endowment for the Humanities, Hally has directed archaeological investigations in the areas of the Richard B. Russell Reservoir and Coosawattee River drainage as well as at the King site. The author of numerous articles and technical reports, he counts among his interests the development of Mississippian sociopolitical systems, ceramic analysis, and prehistoric and historic food procurement and preparation in the Southeast.

Charles Hudson, a professor of anthropology at the University of Georgia, received his Ph.D. degree from the University of North Carolina, Chapel Hill. The preeminent authority on the ethnohistory of the Southeast, he is presently tracing the routes of Hernando de Soto, Tristán de Luna, and Juan Pardo. Hudson edited a volume entitled *Red, White, and Black: Symposium on the Indians of the Old South* (University of Georgia Press, 1971) and wrote the standard reference on native Americans in the region—*The Southeastern Indians* (University of Tennessee Press,

1976). He is senior author of "Coosa: A Chiefdom in the Sixteenth-Century Southeastern United States."

Sharon Kestle earned her B.A. degree in anthropology from Georgia State University in 1986. After a stint with the archaeological firm of Garrow and Associates, Inc., she entered a graduate program in bioarchaeology at Northern Arizona University. Kestle's eclectic interests include genetics, animal ethology, human paleontology, and classical archaeology of the circum-Mediterranean.

David S. Mathews holds an M.A. degree in anthropology from Georgia State University. His master's thesis, "The Battle of Mabila: The Ulibahali Casualties from the King Site," is the first work to link archaeologically recovered native American casualties to a sixteenth-century Spanish expedition in the interior Southeast. Mathews's interests focus on skeletal biology, forensic anthropology, southeastern archaeology, and computer analyses. He is currently employed as an electronic design engineer for a computer software firm in Atlanta.

Marvin Smith received his Ph.D. degree in anthropology from the University of Florida in 1984. He is a research associate of Garrow and Associates, Inc., in Atlanta. Smith's research centers on the ethnohistory of the Southeast, including the response of native Americans to the Spanish presence and the emergence of new sociopolitical alliances in the region. He is the author of *Archaeology of Aboriginal Culture Change: Depopulation During the Early Historic Period* (University of Florida Press, 1987) and coauthored "Coosa: A Chiefdom in the Sixteenth-Century Southeastern United States."

Index

53–55, 59; as part of Coosa
chiefdom, 5; ancestral to
Creek Indians, 47, 54–55,
58–59; relation to Mouse
Creek culture, 48–50,
54–55, 58–59; architecture,
48–49; settlement plan, 49,
53; mortuary treatment,
49–50, 53–54; relation to
Middle Cumberland culture,
54–55, 58–59
Dallas site (Tennessee), 48,
66–67; nutrition at, 71–72;
stature and social status at,
73–74
Demographic theory: population stability and sta-
tionarity, 22, 33 (n. 1). See
also Paleodemography
Dental caries: at King site,
xviii, 64–65, 69–72; and
subsistence, xix, 63–64,
70-72, 75; assessment of,
65–66; and age at King site,
65, 71; between sexes at
King site, 70–72
Dental enamel hypoplasias:
defined, 26; at King and
Etowah sites, 26–28, 32,
96–97; and weaning and disease, 26–28
Dental wear, 63, 67; assessment of, 64–65, 72 (n. 1); at
King site, 67–69, 72; be-
tween sexes at King site,
68–69, 72
De Soto, Hernando, xiv, xx,
42, 119, 122; slave taking,
xx, 112–14, 127–32; responsible for King site massacre,
xx–xxi, 111–16, 124,
129–34; in Coosa chiefdom,
112, 127–30; at Mabila,
112–15, 124–26, 130–32;
route of, 121; use of weapons and dogs, 132, 134
Diagenesis, 66–67
Dickson Mounds site (Illinois): mortality at, 22–25

Diet. See Nutrition
Ditch, 6–10
Dogs: used by Hernando de
Soto, 132, 134
Domestic structures. See
Houses
Domestic zone, 9–11, 13–14,
56. See also Private sector

Enamel hypoplasias. See Dental enamel hypoplasias
Endosteal apposition and resorption. See Cortical bone
thickness
Epidemic diseases. See European diseases; Infectious
diseases
Etowah site (Georgia), 44, 88;
culture, 17, 20; mortality at,
23–29; enamel hypoplasias
at, 26–28, 96–97; subsis-
tence and nutrition at,
26–28, 64–65, 69–72; ar-
tificial cranial deformation
at, 37; dental health at, 64,
69–72; periosteal reactions
at, 91–93, 95, 98; trauma at,
102–3; Hernando de Soto at,
112, 127–28, 130
European artifacts, xiv, xx,
6–7, 40, 57, 114–15, 118,
122
European diseases: unlikely at
King site, 28–29, 96, 98;
bioarchaeological evidence
of, 29, 33 (n. 4), 95–96; in
Southeast, 118. See also Infectious diseases
"European-style" warfare, xx,
110–11, 114
Excavation of King site, 3–5
Exogamy, 55, 59 (n. 3)

Fertility, 17, 22, 31–33. See
also Childbearing
Flathead Indians: artificial cranial deformation among, 37
Fortification. See Palisade

tality at, 18, 20, 22–31, 33–34 (n. 5), 95–96, 103, 105, 111, 114, 116 (n. 1); European diseases unlikely at, 28–29, 96, 98; trace elements at, 32, 71–72, 75; sex roles of residents, 68–72; cortical bone thickness at, 71, 82–86; stature (adult) at, 74
Kinship: at King site, 11, 108–9, 114; among Creek Indians, 55–57
Kwashiorkor, 80

Lamar culture, 5, 11
Laudonnière, René de: expedition of, 118–19
Little Egypt site (Georgia): as capital of Coosa chiefdom, 5, 122; compared with King site, 18, 46. See also Coosa (Georgia)
Lobillo, Johan Ruiz (De Soto captain), 128
Log-lined tombs, 49–51
Luna, Tristán de: expedition of, 119–24; and King site, xiv, 122, 124, 133

Mabila (Alabama) Battle of, xx–xxi, 111, 134; Hernando de Soto at, 112–15, 124–26, 130–31; death toll of, 113, 124; location of, 123–24
Maize, xviii–xix, 26, 63–64, 75
Malnutrition. See Nutrition
Mançano (De Soto soldier), 129
Marriage, 44–45, 55
Massacre of King site residents, xiv, xix–xxi, 102, 105–6, 111–17, 124–26, 129–34. See also Casualties of massacre
Matriliny, 55–56
Mechanical loading: and cor-

tical bone thickness, 81, 84–85
Metropolitan Museum of Art (New York), 6
Middle Cumberland culture, 47; relation to King site, xviii, 53–55, 58–59; settlement plan and architecture, 49; mortuary treatment, 49–51; relation to Mouse Creek culture, 50–51, 58–59; relation to Dallas culture, 54–55, 58–59
Moat. See Ditch
Mortality, 18, 20, 22–31, 33–34 (n. 5), 71, 95–96; and sampling error, 23–25; between sexes, 24, 29–30, 33–34 (n. 5); of massacre victims, 24, 29–30, 103, 104–5, 111, 114, 116 (n. 1); among juveniles, 25–28; among adults, 29–30; between ranks, 30–32
Mortuary treatment: at King site, 15–16, 30–32, 38–45, 49, 53–54, 56–58, 73–74; and social status, 38–39, 73–74, 108; in Dallas, Middle Cumberland, and Mouse Creek cultures, 49–51, 53–54, 74; of massacre victims at King site, 107–9. See also Burials
Mounds, 48–50, 74; absent at King site, 49, 53, 67
Moundville site (Alabama), 35
Mouse Creek culture, 47; relation to King site, xvii, 11, 53–55, 58–59; as part of Coosa chiefdom, 5; settlement plan and architecture, 48–49, 53; relation to Dallas culture, 48–50, 54–55, 58–59; mortuary treatment, 49–51, 53–54; relation to Middle Cumberland culture, 50–51, 58–59

Moyano de Morales, Hernando (Pardo sergeant), 119–20
Muskogean languages, 5, 55

Napochie Indians, 121–24
Natchez Indians, 36
Native Americans, historic: Spanish treatment of, xiv, xx–xxi, 112–14, 119, 122, 124–30, 132; community structure, xvi, xviii, 5–6, 13–14, 112; social organization, xviii, 13, 54–58, 108; physical appearance, 36–37; warfare between, 42–46, 55, 111, 122, 124, 133
Neandertal (Shanidar, Iraq): artificial cranial deformation among, 35
Nutrition: and dental health, xviii–xix, 26–28, 63–64, 70–72; between sexes, xix, 70, 72, 82–83; and health, 27–28, 31, 34 (n. 6); and trace elements, 71–72; and cortical bone thickness, 84–86; and periosteal reactions, 96–98. See also Cortical bone thickness; Subsistence; Trace elements.

Olameco (Tennessee), 119
Osteoporosis. See Cortical bone thickness

Paleodemography, xvi, 33 (nn. 2, 3); of King site, xvi–xvii; uses of, 17, 32; sampling error and, 23–25. See also Demographic theory
Palisade, 42–43, 46 (n. 1); at King site, 6, 9–10, 133
Pardo, Juan: expedition of, 119–21, 134
Pathology. See Skeletons
Periodontal disease, 71
Periosteal reactions: and

wounds, xv, xix–xx, 87–88, 91–94, 96, 98, 105, 114; and infectious diseases, xv, 87–88, 95–98; and nutrition, xv, 96–98; at King site, xv–xvi, xix–xx, 91–98; defined, 87–88; assessment of, 90–91; between ages and sexes at King site, 92–93, 96, 98
Peruvian Indians: artificial cranial deformation among, 37
Piache (Alabama), 112
Piachi (Georgia), 123; as possible King site, 128; Hernando de Soto at, 128–29
Plaza, 49–50, 53; at King site, 6, 9, 14–15, 56–57. See also Public sector
Porotic hyperostosis, 26, 28
Potts Tract site (Georgia), 5; compared with King site, 18
Preagriculturalists. See Gathering and hunting
Private sector, 18–20, 30–32, 39–41, 44, 57–58, 73–74, 95. See also Domestic zone
Protein-calorie malnutrition (PCM), 79–81
Public sector, 18–20, 30–32, 38–39, 42–44, 56–57, 73–74, 95. See also Plaza

Rank. See Status (social)
Research design: for study of King site skeletons, xv–xvi
Robles (black slave), 128–29

Santa Elena (South Carolina), 119
Settlement plan, xvi–xviii, 6–16, 18–19; relation to burials, 15–16; of contemporaneous cultures, 49, 53
Sex determination of skeletons, 20–21, 45
Sex ratio, 21, 33–34 (n. 5); be-

Index